12 CASE STU [illegible] MENT INTERVENTION AND DOCUMENTATION EXAMPLES FOR OCCUPATIONAL THERAPISTS WORKING IN SKILLED NURSING FACILITIES

- ☞ Case studies
- ☞ Documentation examples
- ☞ Real testimonial stories
- ☞ Tips to motivate challenging patients
- ☞ and much more….

ISBN-13: 978-0-578-43576-3
ISBN-10: 0-578-43576-4

Disclaimer: The material found in this book is concise; all experience and ideas are solely those of the author's imagination, otherwise specified and referenced. The patient names mentioned are considered fictional, any resemblance to persons, living or dead, is entirely coincidental and only used to simulate real case issues. This is supportive material for occupational students and licensed therapists and is only meant as supplemental information, not a substitution of accredited institutional education.

Reference:

American Occupational Therapy Association. (2014). Occupational therapy practice framework: Domain & process (3rd ed.). American Journal of Occupational Therapy, 68(Suppl. 1), S1–S48. http://dx.doi.org/10.5014/ajot.2014.682006

Early, M. B. (2006). Physical dysfunction practice skills for the occupational therapy assistant. St. Louis, MO: Mosby Elsevier.

Reviewers

Grea Alegre, OTR/L, DOR
Tracy Loncke, OTR/L
Amanda Bush COTA/L

Dedication

I want to thank my family, husband, peers, followers, and patients who inspired me to write this book. I have seen some amazing recoveries and also had my share of losses, but through it all being an occupational therapy assistant is rewarding. I hope with my experiences, I can help new grads and seasoned therapists have a better perspective of quality treatment, documentation, and a better understanding of the multi diagnoses we see daily.

Table of Contents

Selected Abbreviation for Medicine and Rehabilitation*

AAROM	Active assisted range of motion
ADL	Activities of daily living
AFO	Ankle-foot orthosis
AROM	Active range of motion
AE	Adaptive equipment
AD	Assistive device
AKA	Above-knee amputation
BP	Blood pressure
(B)UE	Bilateral (both) upper extremity
BOS	Base of support
(B)LE	Bilateral (both) lower extremity
b/l	Bilateral
BKA	Below-knee amputation
CHF	Congestive heart failure
CABG	Coronary artery bypass graft
COC	Cocaine
COPD	Chronic obstructive pulmonary disease
CHD	Congenital heart disease
c/o	Complaint of
CVA	Cerebrovascular accident (stroke)
d/t	Due to
D/C or d/c	Discharge
DOB	Date of birth
Demo	Demonstrated
Dx or dx	Diagnosis
DVT	Deep vein thrombosis
EOB	Edge of bed
E/C	Energy conservation
ETOH	Ethyl alcohol
FWB	Full weight bearing

FMC	Fine motor control
f/u	Follow-up
CGA	Contact guard assist
HTN	Hypertension
HHA	Handheld assist
HOH	Hard of hearing *or* Hand over hand assist (depends on usage)
Hx	History
HR	Heart rate
(I)	Independent
LOB	Loss of balance
LHS	Long handle sponge
LTC	Long-term care
LE	Lower extremity
(L)UE	Left upper extremity
MI	Myocardial infraction
MHP	Moist hot pack
MD	Medical doctor
MMT	Manual muscle test
Mod (I)	Modified independent
Min A	Minimal assistance
Mod A	Moderate assistance
Max A	Maximum assistance
MCP	Metacarpophalangeal
NC	Nasal cannula
OA	Osteoarthritis
OOB	Out of bed
PLOF	Prior level of function
PAM	Physical agent modalities
PICC	Peripherally inserted central catheter
PVD	Peripheral vascular disease
Pt	Patient
QOL	Quality of life
ROM	Range of motion

RW	Rolling walker
(R)UE	Right upper extremity
R*eps*	Repetition
s/p	Status post
S	Supervision
SOB	Shortness of breath
SROM	Self-range of motion
STE	Steps to enter
SNF	Skilled nursing facility
SPT	Stand pivot transfer
SPC	Single point cane
TED	Thrombo-embolic deterrent
UE	Upper extremity
UTI	Urinary tract infection
UB	Upper body
vc's	Verbal cues
WFL	Within functional limits
WNL	Within normal limits
w/	With
WBAT	Weight-bearing as tolerated
w/c	Wheelchair
w/o	Without
y/o	Year old

Balance Scale Simplified

Balance Code	Abbreviation	Simplified definition
Normal	N	Patient **independently** maintains balance against strong resistance, moving outside base of support in multiple directions without assistive device.
Good	G	Patient **supervised** during moderate balance resistance, moving outside base of support in multiple directions without assistive device.
Good-	G-	Patient maintains balance with **close supervision** without assistive device during minimal balance challenges outside base of support.
Fair +	F+	Patient can maintain static stand unsupported, however requires **contact guard assistance** during balance challenging activities outside base of support.
Fair	F	Patient **requires the use of assistive device** during dynamic movements within base of support, unable to tolerate resistance and balance challenges.
Fair-	F-	Patient requires **Min A** to maintain balance with the use of assistive device, and cannot tolerate any balance challenges.

Poor +	P+	Patient requires **Mod A** to maintain balance with use of assistive device, cannot tolerate any balance challenges.
Poor	P	Patient requires **Max Ax1-2 person** to maintain balance with the use of assistive device, and cannot tolerate any balance challenges.
Unable	Unable	Patient cannot support him/herself, **totally dependent**, usually requires hoyer lift for transfers

Manual Muscle Scale Simplified

Number	Letters	Description
Against gravity (Active movement)		
5	N (normal)	Full movement of extremity, muscle holds joint against strong pressure
4	G (good)	Full movement of extremity, muscle holds joint against moderate pressure
4-	G-	Full movement of extremity, muscle holds joint against minimal pressure
3+	F+	Full movement of extremity, capable of slight pressure, but collapses abruptly.
3	F (fair)	Full movement of extremity but unable to tolerate resistance, muscle holds test position, no added pressure
3-	F-	Less than full range of motion of extremity, unable to tolerate resistance, gradual release from test position
Gravity lessened position (supported movement)		
2+	Poor+	Full extremity movement in supported position, then releases/breaks held position upon minimal pressure
2	P (poor)	Full extremity movement in supported position, however no added resistance
2-	P-	Less than full range of motion in

		supported position
1	T (trace)	No visible movement, but can feel muscle contraction
0	0 (zero)	No movement, no contraction

Introduction

Thank you for investing in my book. I have been an occupational therapy assistant for 6+ years. I would like to share how I got started. I am going to take you back in time to when I first discovered Occupational Therapy and why I decided to close down my hair studio and move to New Jersey. My journey started at Quinsigamond Community College in Worcester, MA and finished in Dobbs Ferry, NY at Mercy College. Here is my word for word essay I wrote for acceptance into the occupational therapy profession. I started with one of my most inspired, yet favorite quote. "The future was uncertain, absolutely, and there were many hurdles, twists, and turns to come, but as long as I kept moving forward, one foot in front of the other, the voices of fear and shame, the messages from those who wanted me to believe that I wasn't good enough, would be stilled."
_ Chris Gardner, The Pursuit of Happiness

I will never forget my first. The first time I sat in the Worcester College auditorium, sectioned off into groups like pieces of a puzzle waiting for its rightful place. I sat beside my father anticipating the outcome of the day. The thought of college seemed surreal. The sweat from my brow got in the way as I looked around the room imagining university life, but I was quickly snapped back into reality once the speaker announced, "all here for occupational therapy please move to my far right." "What is Occupational Therapy?" I thought to myself as I felt a tug on my forearm. It was my father collecting our belongings, reminding me about the purpose of our trip: the nursing program. I did not want to be a nurse; however, I entertained the idea for my father's sake. After minutes of convincing, debating, and back and forth suggestions, my father accompanied me ten rows to the far right. I was captivated by the speaker. Her message was straightforward and motivating, "Occupational Therapist helps people find tools and strategies they need to overcome barriers, such as illness and disabilities in order to reach their goals in life". What a simple, yet interesting concept. The room felt still, overwhelmed with emotion. I thought "That's it! I want to be an Occupational Therapist." Some people would say there is no such thing as love at first sight but for me, this was it. I believe when you are constantly soul-searching, the complexities of life can throw you off track, but once you have that moment of clarity, you must act.

My Journey began; surfing the internet, www.salary.com, YouTube videos, leaving voicemails at rehabilitation hospitals and skilled nursing facilities. I was determined to reinforce my desire and had to confirm to myself that this is really what I wanted. Whittier Rehabilitation Hospital in Westborough, MA welcomed me for a two-day observation with an Occupational Therapist. Astounded by her holistic approach and professional demeanor, it was clear she loved her job. I was convinced. My application was submitted and I was on my way. Unfortunately, the road was narrow and rough. Due to financial hardship, I had to apply to a community college in order to keep my job and help my family.

Quinsigamond Community College required a Test of Essential Academic Skills (TEAS) for admission into a healthcare program. TEAS scores must be achieved within two attempts for acceptance into the Occupational Therapy Assistant (OTA) Program. The TEAS test is a four-part, web-based, supervised assessment that includes subtests in Reading, Mathematics, Science, and English language usage. English has always been an uphill battle after leaving my home in South America. Every hair on my body was upright, my heart pounded, and the feeling of turning corkscrews sent my stomach into a frenzy. I signed in and sat down. I heard every click, sigh, and pin drop as I continuously glimpsed at the running clock on the computer screen. I fell short by three points. This happened twice in the same category, English. At that moment, my heart sunk and defeat slammed into me in like a flood. I read the dreaded words "Sorry, you were not accepted. The advi-

sor stated, "This was just not meant for you. Do you have other options?" Fighting with every ounce of strength to hold back tears, I could not fathom recalculating my journey. I was mentally invested and not ready to admit defeat. Perseverance means to me, the greater the obstacle, the greater the glory in overcoming it. I pleaded with the advisor and had no intent to leave her office without proper counsel. There was no room for a plan B. I was directed to speak with the Director of the Occupational therapy program. She recognized my determination, but unfortunately, she did not have the final decision. Again, I was redirected to the Dean of health care. After my compelling argument, the Dean stated, "We have never let anyone into the occupational therapy assistant program three points short of the required TEAS score. You are a rare case. I will give you a chance". Regardless of my strict work schedule, I showed up every day to see my English tutor.

Finally, I completed my tutoring and received my acceptance letter. The expected enthusiasm was altered by shame and fear. I did not feel equal to my peers because of my prior process. It is truly sad how self-doubt can impact your self-esteem. I juggled late nights, bloodshot eyes, overwhelming highlighter fumes and running into work a minute before my clock in time to succeed in school. The day of graduation, I was on cloud nine. I reflected on my college journey, from entering the OTA program feeling valueless to then graduating top of my class, earning the Rose Capriolli Memorial Award (an award for an OTA student who consistently demonstrated excellence both in the classroom and clinical settings). Soon after, I passed my NBCOT exam. The experience was worth every drop of the blood, sweat, and tears that went into completing the program. I have reached my happiness. Failure is not an option, hope forever. I have seen patients come into my facility totally dependent, but leave walking on their own. The joy this has brought to my life, words cannot express.

I want to influence every person under my care to live life to the fullest, regardless of disability, illness, or injury. Holding a comb, turning a cap and moving a finger are steps towards recovery. As a therapist, life momentarily regains a sense of potential, feeling of awe, gratitude, and pride to discover what has made the process easier and quicker for your patients. This profession needs innovation, regeneration, and entrepreneurship. This profession needed me. I believe knowledge is power, information is liberating and education is the premise of progress. I want to write scholarly evidence-based literature, invent new adaptive equipment and most of all succeed. This is why I have chosen Occupational Therapy as my career.

Looking back at this essay, I was so passionate. I knew what I wanted, went after it, and succeeded. So the doors of my hair studio had closed and my new life was wrapped around being an occupational therapy assistant. I moved from Massachusetts to be closer to my husband whom at the time was my boyfriend. So fast forward, what happened to my passion for occupational therapy? I believe so many people have experienced moments like this in their life. You expected one thing but life spits out another. I planned on going back to school for my master's degree which I did, but decided to graduate with my bachelors in Health Science due to the expense and second-guessing the worth and benefits of continuing. I had rent, bills, and an upcoming wedding to think about.

I then made the decision to start my own business and get out of the "rat race". I wanted to be done with a 9 to 5 job. My first attempt to become an independent business person was through creating an invention. I created an adaptive equipment for occupational therapy, getting as far as the 3-D prototype. I was unable to complete this mission due to the financial burden. I decided to take a risk and jump, but my parachute did not open.

This first failure was not only frustrating but I admit it was poorly researched. I did not realize the steps required to invent, market, and patent a product, not to mention the legalities. The amount of money required to patent my product was not worth it at the time, furthermore, I was uncertain on how successful it would be. Can I financially sustain this investment? I questioned my creativity and vision and the time it would take to complete the process. I, then impatiently came up with a website idea, surely this will be safer.

This is when myOTcares.com was born. I wanted so bad to have my own business. I convinced myself to stay within my profession since I invested so much time, effort, and money in my college experience. I couldn't just throw it all away. Even though this may have caught you off guard, I truly believe everyone wants to leave behind their mark, his or her legacy, something to be proud of, of value. I have decided to become an OT consultant. I will continue to help others, answer questions and work until the time is right. I am moving towards bigger and better things. My new organization called iRIZE, LLC is a self-improvement and development service. I chose not to limit myself but provide a service that not only benefits rehabilitation patients, but everyone.

Well, I guess I am still trying to help individuals reach their highest quality of life, the OT in me will never die. So I have made the decision to leave behind my most effective treatment ideas, tips, documentation examples, and how to's that gain the highest level of results that any therapist can apply now. This book also contains my most used abbreviations section, testimonials, and more. So I suggest you continue reading. The profession is changing, budget cuts and insurance limitations are putting more demands on therapists and the rehabilitation process. A simple tip can make a huge difference and besides, sharing is caring. I hope this book will be a great assistance for new graduates and seasoned therapists needing a refresher.

How to use this book?

This book can be used as a quick reference after reading the introduction and skipping to the diagnosis of choice or read from beginning to the end. Please review the often used abbreviation page as a reference prior to chapter 1. I suggest overlooking the abbreviations, balance, and manual muscle scale in order to have a full grasp of the therapeutic dialogue, numbers, letters, and usage. I have provided 12 diagnoses that are often seen in skilled nursing facilities. Each case study will have the patient's name and ailment followed by a brief review of their given treatment diagnosis. The brief review will provide a short explanation and insight into the given diagnosis as a quick reference.

The profile introduces the patient and their case. I have created a mini version of what you will actually see on an evaluation. It will provide patient history and any complexities in the patient's case such as high blood pressure, chronic illness, old injuries etc. As you continue under patient profile, you will also be provided with precautions (preventative measures and cautions) to be aware of, prior level of function (patient's performance prior to illness, injury or disability), assessment & underlying impairment (current level of functioning, observation and measurements) and lastly skill justification (why is skilled OT services required and planned goal for attainment). Next, the treatment sections are tips and treatment ideas that can be applied now. The given treatments can be applied to multiple diagnoses. I have and continue to use these treatment ideas in my practice. It is all about being creative while facilitating a functional outcome for your patient that can be carried over upon discharge home.

Some of the treatments I am sure you already use, but I hope to enhance your outlook and interaction with your patient. Lastly, documentation with billing treatment codes. The basic billing treatment codes for Medicare used in skilled nursing facilities are 97166 for occupational therapy evaluation. Let's assume the evaluation was completed, the code added, and the information we have is the patient's profile. The treatment codes mentioned in this book are therapeutic exercise 97110, neuro re-education 97112, therapeutic activities 97530, self-care training 97535, and wheelchair management 97542. Specialty billing codes are 97760 for orthotic training (splints), 97018 for paraffin bath therapy and many more that I will not reference in this book. After you have reviewed and/or completed the patient's profile, also known as evaluation, it is time to create your short and long-term goals, plan your treatment sessions and document your observation, measurements, subjective, and patient status. You will notice I have written my short term and long term goals in many different ways in order to provide you with a well-rounded outlook on how to word your goals or what you may see. These goals will guide your planned treatment sessions. Usually, you will have your patient for 45-60 minutes, 5 days a week for a duration of 41 weeks until recertification assessment.

As a COTA or OTR, it is your goal to progress your patients to achieve their goals within a reasonable timeframe in order to create new goals of increased complexity to facilitate prior level of functioning. Please keep in mind a normal evaluation will have more detail, but this is simply a shorter version I have put together for you. I did not mention a functional test, but all evaluations should contain one. To conclude, I have added some of my favorite therapeutic exercises for upper extremity strengthening and functional goal attainment. Lastly, my rebuttal for motivating the unmotivated patient to participate in therapy. If this book has helped you in any way please share with your fellow co-worker, classmate, and educator.

Roles of OTs in SNF

It is important to understand your role as an occupational therapist in a skilled nursing setting. According to AOTA, occupational therapy practitioners focus on "achieving health, wellbeing, and participation in life through engagement in occupation". We must train our patient's in self-care skills (ADLs), use of adaptive equipment, compensatory techniques, environmental modifications, IADLs while dealing with behavioral and mental health issues. In addition to planning the patient's discharge environment. Occupational therapists instruct in meal preparation, housekeeping, energy conservation techniques, work simplification strategies, management of one's home or finances, community reintegration (as appropriate for the client's discharge site) with activities such as public dining or emergency response management, assessing and recommending potential home modifications, safety equipment to reduce barriers and decrease the risk of falls. Occupational therapists introduce compensatory strategies for return to volunteer or paid employment, leisure, functional mobility with or without ambulatory device for transfers to different surfaces, such as a bed, chair, toilet, or shower in order to perform self-care and personal tasks; wheelchair mobility and management, training in the ability to use the telephone or the emergency staff call bell.

Therapists also teach patients with cognitive and perceptual deficits in compensatory techniques to maximize abilities in areas such as attention span, orientation, sequencing and memory. Patient's function with low vision are taught how to maximize their remaining vision and enhance safety through compensatory techniques, environmental modifications, assistive technology, and adaptive equipment. Occupational therapists develop fall preventions, dementia management, restraint reduction, contracture management, and positioning programs to name a few in order to ensure the safety of short and long-term patients.

Just as important as it is to know the role of occupational therapists in an SNF setting, it is also important to know the roles of OTR vs COTAs. According to AOTA, only OTRs can evaluate, develop a plan of care, complete recertification, and discharge patients. They can delegate selected assessments to COTAs based on competency and if permitted by state law, but OTRs are responsible for evaluations, g-codes for Medicare part B patients and goals. COTAs always work under the supervision of an OTR although they can treat and document independently while contributing to progress notes, recertification, and discharges as permitted by state law and other applicable regulations.

OTRs responsibilities includes documentation of standardized functional tests on evaluation, creation of short and long-term goals with frequency, duration and treatment modalities included, daily treatment documentation, weekly progress reports, screens, recertification, completing functional status update forms for insurance companies, creating care plans for nursing, attending caregiver or discharge meetings, completing billing logs, educating and training students and supervising/co-signing assistant therapists documentation. COTAs have similar responsibilities as OTRs within a SNF such as providing comprehensive treatment to patients under supervision of an OTR according to state guidelines, assist in identifying appropriate rehab candidates, document daily notes, document progress notes, assist with patient recertification and discharge recommendations, attend caregiver and discharge meetings, participate in utilization review meetings, complete billing logs, conduct in-services, train and educate student OTAs with state OT board regulations and requirements and much more. I know you will benefit from this book. I appreciate all feedback. If you are in need of a speaker for your next upcoming event please contact me at Timisha.daniels@gmail.com. Enjoy!

Chapter 1
Case Study 1: Hoffman, George
Cerebral Vascular Accident (stroke)

Brief Review:

Terminology

- Stroke: a sudden loss of blood supply to the brain.
- Hemorrhagic stroke: also known as a hemorrhage, a ruptured blood vessel resulting in bleeding into the brain.
- Transient ischemic attack: known as "TIA", is an incomplete stroke which is classified as temporary with quick recovery.
- Ischemic stroke: caused by a thrombus (blood clot) or embolus (moving blood clot). An ischemic stroke is a slow bleed whereas hemorrhagic is a quick bleed which is more deadly. The right hemisphere controls the left side of the body and the left hemisphere controls the right side of the body. It is good to understand that when there is a left CVA, language (aphasia) and motor movements (apraxia) are affected whereas if it's a right CVA, a person's visual and perception is affected.
- Hemiplegia: one side paralysis and often seen unilateral neglect
- Hemiparesis: partial motor loss, weakness
- Aspiration- food, and liquids that travel to the lungs instead of the stomach
- Dysphagia- difficulty swallowing
- Dysphasia- inability to express oneself
- Dysarthria- decreased coordination of facial muscles, high tone

- Apraxia- unable to motor plan
- Dyspraxia- difficulty motor planning
- Agnosia- decreased ability to recognize objects with vision or touch
- Diplopia- double vision
- Aphasia- language disorder, difficulty with verbal expression
- Anomia- difficulty with word finding

As a therapist, it is important to educate your patients and caregivers on the signs and symptoms of a stroke. You will want to look for sudden numbness in the face, arms and legs on one side, difficulty speaking or understanding, difficulty seeing, difficulty walking, dizziness, loss of balance, severe headache, nausea and vomiting, loss of consciousness, and high blood pressure.

Patient Profile:

History/Complexities:
Mr. George Hoffman, age 71, and gender male admitted with a diagnosis of left hemisphere CVA resulting in right side hemiparesis. Patient has a history of HTN, falls, and epilepsy.

Precautions: falls, seizure, foley catheter, and aspiration

Prior level of function (PLOF):
Patient lives with his nephew and was independent with ADLs. Patient performed functional mobility independently without AD prior to CVA. Pt currently requires maximum assistance for upper body dressing and transfers. The patient is totally dependent for toileting and bathing. Patient requires moderate assistance for feeding, hygiene & grooming, and bed mobility.

Assessment & Underlying impairment:

- Impaired FMC
- Impaired safety awareness, +1 edema right UE
- Fair-static sitting balance
- Poor static standing balance
- Right upper extremity ROM impaired
- (R)UE muscular strength 2/5

Skilled justification:

Patient requires skilled OT services to facilitate independence with ADLs, minimize safety hazards/barriers by increasing safety awareness, maximize rehab potential, facilitate sitting tolerance, improve postural control, improve fine motor coordination and strength in upper extremities in order to enhance patient's QOL by increasing independence and safety with basic ADLs, functional transfers and mobility.

Mr. Hoffman's goals

Short term:

1. Patient will increase (R)UE strength to 3-/5 in order to improve (I) with UB dressing utilizing e-stim modalities and strength training as appropriate.
2. Patient will complete hygiene and grooming (brushing teeth, wash face, comb hair) tasks seated in w/c requiring Min A and 50% verbal/tactile to establish compensatory technique in order to perform basic ADLs with increased independence and safety.
3. Patient will increase static sitting balance during ADLs to fair+ in order to reduce the risk of falls during EOB activities.

Long term:

1. Patient will complete all aspect of hygiene/grooming (brush teeth, wash face, comb hair) tasks seated in w/c supervised utilizing one hand technique to perform BADLs.

Treatment interventions & Tips:

1. Sleeping positions

   Instruct patient in proper sleeping position with the use of pillows to decrease increased (R)UE/LE edema and abnormal body alignment. Your patient may be a side sleeper and prefer to be in this position. It is recommended that your patient sleeps on their non-effected side with the use of pillows.

   On side

   1st assist your patient to roll on to their non-effected side with a pillow positioned under their head.

   2nd place a pillow behind their back to prevent rolling backward.

   3rd place 1-2 pillows under their affected arm so that the shoulder is slightly forward and hand is supported. I like to make sure my patient's hand is not hanging over the pillow.

   4th place 1-2 pillows between their legs with unaffected leg straight and affected leg forward with knee and hip slightly flexed. This is the ideal way to position a stroke patient.

   On back:

   1st put a pillow behind their head (centrally positioned).

   2nd place a pillow under their affected arm (scapula protracted) ensuring the pillow is under their shoulder

to decrease the risk of subluxation at the joint and pain from lack of support.
3rd place a pillow between their leg and bed rail to prevent external rotation of hip to facilitate proper body alignment. I would advise you to train the patient's CNA on bed positioning to facilitate adequate carryover.

2. Weight shifting at EOB
    1st assist patient to EOB sitting, feet flat on floor and hands on the bed for self-support.
    2nd instruct in forward and backward weight shifting. You should be in front of your patient seated on a swivel chair, don't forget to use proper body mechanics.
    3rd support their affected UE, focusing on elbow and hand to create a fluidity and controlled movement to decrease patient fear of falling forward. You can also assist their trunk from collapsing during trunk flexion and extension.

3. Lateral weight shifting at EOB with purpose
    - Instruct your patient in lateral weight shifting using their unaffected UE to retrieve items off their bedside table such as lotion, deodorant, comb, cell phone, crossing midline to place into their bag or basin which will be positioned beside their affected UE on the bed.

4. Modified sit to stand training
    For this activity, your patient will be seated in their w/c.
    1st carefully ace wrap their affected hand to the w/c armrest.
    2nd position yourself in front of your patient supporting their affected leg (knee) with your knee. If this is un-

comfortable for your patient simple fold a towel and place between your knee and theirs.

3rd place your hands on their hips to control their pelvic movement or use a gait belt.

4th with one leg forward, shift your weight backward while maintaining proper body mechanics as you assist your patient into a mid-way stand until the elbows are straight, then guide them back into their w/c. You are not doing a complete stand. This activity provides weight bearing, weight shifting, and neuromuscular re-education while maintaining control of the affected UE.

- Using ace bandage to wrap patient's affected hand on to parallel bar (not to tight, bearable) perform complete sit to stand while supporting weaker side.

5. Basic ADL training
    - Have patient place lotion on the body, tactile feedback during self-care.
    - Use brushing technique for tactile feedback of affected extremity.
    - Instructed in sequential dressing first the affected UE extremity, then the unaffected UE extremity, followed by pulling overhead, lastly adjusting sides, front and back using unaffected UE.
    - Tie a piece of theraband together, knot at ends, place affected extremity through an opening in order to train in simulated donning/doffing of shirt sleeve with focus on management, grasp, one-hand technique, and coordination.
    - Instruct patient with the use of AE (reacher or dressing stick) as needed in order to don/doff pants or simply instruct your patient in cross leg technique by using

their non-affected extremity to cross their affected leg in order to donn pants, socks, and shoes. I would recommend loose-fitting clothing, socks, and shoes with velcro, slip-on or elastic laces.

- Instruct on the use of dressing stick for jackets and open front garments

6. Mirror activity (visual-feedback for postural control) Depending on patient's sitting balance, they can either be in their w/c or on therapy mat.

   1st position a long mirror in front of your patient. You should be positioned on their affected side with their affected UE supporting themselves.

   2nd instruct your patient to write with unaffected UE either their name or numbers 1-5, using window washable markers, grade activity accordingly.

   3rd have your patient support themselves using the unaffected UE while you provide the least amount of assistance to erase each letter or number one-by-one with affected UE. You can grade this activity accordingly to make it easier or more difficult.

   - Pt seated, therapist standing behind, long mirror vertically placed centered to patient with (L) hand on back of mirror while (R) hand on mirror, elbows flexed at 90 degrees, instruct in guidance of both hands up/down mirror.

7. Strength & ROM training

   This treatment tip is dependent on the patient's affected UE strength. Usually patients with hemiparesis are able to do this seated in their w/c, however, this therapeutic exercise can be conducted in a gravity lessened position which is in supine.

1st place yellow theraband through therapy cone opening and make a knot.
2nd Place your patient's affected on top of the cone.
3rd hold the knotted end of the theraband to assist with lifting their extremity as you instruct them to push down. This can be 10 repetition x 3 sets or more, you be the judge.

- SROM and HHA therapeutic exercises are also beneficial
- Depends on hand strength, wrist weights
- AA/AROM as appropriate
- Isometric exercises

    1st seated on the therapy mat, guide the patient on to forearm (affected) laterally.
    2nd instruct the patient to push off their elbow, extending the arm, sitting upright, return back to mat and repeat.

- Strap affected UE on to arm skateboard while seated, move in all shoulder planes, grade accordingly.
- Incorporate E-stim modalities (must be certified in PAM)

8. Bilateral integration grasp training activity
The patient is seated in w/c with hi-lo table positioned in front.

    1st patient's arms are on the table with elbow supported. You may need to assist your patient's affected UE on to the table and hand in a mildly fisted position.
    2nd place a therapy cone, foam tube or marker near the patient's unaffected side.
    3rd instruct the patient to pick up each item one-by-one and place into their affected hand with attention on grasp/release response to hold items without dropping in preparation for hygiene/grooming, grade accordingly.

Every patient is different so you will have to modify your treatments accordingly. So here is the big question, how do you document your treatment session to receive full reimbursement through their insurance? I have provided you with two examples.

Documentation:

Neuro Re-Ed: 97112

1. Patient instructed in static sitting balance seated on therapy mat with focus on trunk control, bilateral UE weight bearing and righting reactions displaying fair-balance with moderate verbal and tactile cueing to facilitate upright sitting posture in w/c and during self-care tasks.

Self-Care: 97535

2. Patient instructed in UB dressing training donning/doffing t-shirt (theraband simulation) implementing one-hand technique after verbal and visual demonstration to facilitate proper sequencing and safety requiring Min/Mod A + 50% verbal and tactile cues for task completion during return demonstration.

Testimonial 1: Charlie 2-month post stroke

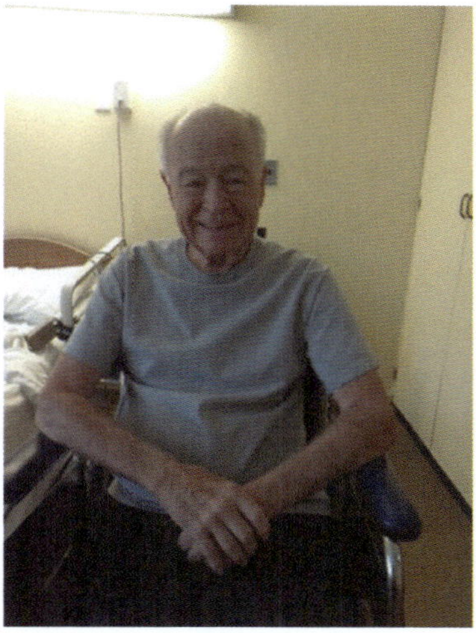

"Good morning, my name is Charles Graham. On October 9th of this year 2016 I had a debilitating stroke and went to the hospital and at that time I could not sit up or raise my arm and things like that. I remember very little about it, but my wife fills me in on what I couldn't do. I have come to therapy to rectify some of that. One of the therapists I have worked with is Timisha (Daniels) Tross. She has worked on my ability to use my right hand which at the time of the stroke I couldn't raise over my head, now I can and my right leg along with walking with the aim of getting me back home. Maybe not a 100% as how I was before, but at least able to take care of myself. I am retired and my wife is retired and I have to be able to do that in order to get home. I have found Ms. Daniels to be superb and competent and because of her and others, I have been able to regain a lot of my ability to move, to walk, to use my hand and to actually live. So I thank her and all the other therapists that worked with me because even though it is slow, it is working. Thank you"

---Charles Graham

Case Study 2: Puma, John
Dementia

Brief Review:

Dementia is the loss of mental functions caused by changes in the brain such as memory, reasoning, thinking, and personality changes are often seen. It is a degenerative disease of the nervous system that unfortunately does not have a cure. Dementia is associated with Alzheimer's disease. The life expectancy of an Alzheimer patient is about 7 years. Behavioral symptoms that a therapist would often see is depression, agitation, wandering, delusions, hallucinations, insomnia, and anxiety. Many patients tend to live in the past. Some key signs of early Dementia/Alzheimer disease are memory lapse, forgetting familiar words, misplacing objects, word or name-finding difficulty, poor reading retention, decrease in the ability to plan or organize and poor concentration.

I have listed some key ways to communicate with a dementia patient.

- Approach calmly, from the front with a smile.
- Stand to one side of the person, so they do not feel trapped
- Establish eye contact.
- Do not stand over the patient, remain at their eye level so they do not feel inferior.
- Introduce yourself by name.
- Use the person's name instead of calling them "honey" or "sweetheart".
- Be careful with your emotions, they can pick up on it easily.
- Don't take things too personal, since dementia patients go through personality changes.
- Speak slowly.

- Use low pitched tone, don't yell. You may need to raise your voice if they are short of hearing.
- Use as few words as possible.
- Use visual and gesture cues such as pointing to the bathroom before going there.
- Allow time for the person to respond.
- Repeat your requests exactly the same way and tone if the person does not respond the first time.

Patient Profile:

History/Complexities:
Mr. John Puma age 85, gender male, admitted with a diagnosis of UTI and dementia. His daughter was called by the patient's neighbor because the patient was found wandering in the hallway at 1 am in the morning, unable to find his apartment, frantic and had a high smell of urine. The patient was sent for skilled OT services for UTI and deteriorating (moderate) cognitive impairment. Patient has a history UTI, dehydration, dementia, hypokalemia (low potassium).

Precautions: falls, dementia

Prior level of function (PLOF):
Patient lives alone in an apartment on the 1st floor with elevator and 4 stairs to enter the apartment building. The patient was independent with functional mobility w/o AD and all ADLs. D/c location to be addressed is dependent on therapy assessment/recommendation, possible d/c to this LTC facility.

Assessment & Underlying impairment:
- Follows 1-2 step directions
- CGA for UB dressing, CGA/Min A for toileting, Min A for LB dressing

- Impaired safety awareness, oriented to person
- FMC intact, sensory processing intact
- Static sitting balance normal, dynamic sitting balance good, dynamic standing balance fair +
- (B)UE is WFL, (B)UE strength 4-/5

Skilled justification:
Patient requires skilled OT services to assess safety and independence with ADLs, increase safety awareness, maximize rehab potential, assess and modify environmental hazards and barriers while conducting caregiver training to facilitate highest functional level and patient safety.

Mr. Puma's goals

Short term:

1. Patient will safely perform all aspect of toileting using standard commode with CGA and verbal cues for implementation of safety techniques.
2. Patient will safely and efficiently perform UB dressing (S) to improve sequencing and proper carryover of the task to achieve independence.
3. Patient will access room within facility 2/3 trials with minimal verbal cues with the least amount of environmental barriers.

Long term:

1. Patient will safely perform all aspect of toileting using standard commode (S) with occasional verbal cues to ensure safety and proper sequencing.
2. Patient will access room within facility 3/3 trials (S) with occasional verbal cues as needed.

Treatment interventions & Tips:

The best treatment ideas for patients with moderate dementia is procedural memory tasks. In Mr. Puma's case, we will focus on ADLs (toileting, dressing and finding his room).

1. UB dressing in 1-2-3 steps

    When putting on a t-shirt (I would remain from using garments with buttons at this time)

    1st put left arm through shirt sleeve
    2nd put right arm through shirt sleeve
    3rd use both hands to pull shirt overhead

    - You can have the patient sing the steps.
    - You can have your patient repeat the steps as you provide HHA for proper sequencing. You can grade this task according to your patient's needs and functional level.
    - It is crucial that you are consistent with your words and steps. When training your patient to take off their shirt, say the same sequence in reverse. You would have to use your clinical reasoning skills to assess if it is appropriate to perform donning and doffing of their t-shirt within the same session or split donning and doffing training. You do not want to overload your patient with information.

    UB dressing with pictures

    - Simply print out colored pictures from the internet of someone donning/doffing their shirt. Pictures are often good cues to support success.

    UB dressing in front of the mirror

- Positioning your patient in front of a mirror while you guide in sequential dressing. I would refrain from using AE.
  *Remember this person has been performing this activity throughout their life, so it will be somewhat familiar.

2. Therapeutic Activity
   Color matching activities
   1st get a large poster board.
   2nd draw 8 medium circles.
   3rd color in each circle with a different color.
   4th repeat steps 1-3 with another poster board, but cut out these circles.
   5th place sticky velcro behind each cut out circle and use this as your matching repetitive activity.

3. Recall training: Use identification images, ex. Place a picture of a toilet on the bathroom door.
   - You will instruct your patient to match the colors; to improve attention to task, problem solving, and repetition (memory training).

4. Realistic tasks
   Find out more about your patient's history. What was their profession, likes, and hobbies? For example:
   If Mr. Puma enjoys a clean house. Some treatment tasks you can implement are:
   - Sweeping (repetitive activity)
   - Folding shirts
   - Wiping mirror or table

5. No more wandering

1st place a red balloon or bright red circle on patient's door. It is a good idea to find out from the family if the patient has a favorite color because this can provide a symbolic meaning.
2nd walk with your patient through the hallway, some patients prefer to hold hands as a sense of security. (Keep distance short, do not go around the building or unit)
3rd stop at each corner or turn, give your patient time to process what they see before proceeding.
4th Limit conversation or distraction. Remind them to look for a red balloon or red circle on a door.

- In order to simplify your patient's environment use signs, doors, and lighting, but keep it to a limit. This activity should be repeated with family members and caregivers to facilitate carryover and familiarity.

6. Therapeutic exercise

- Some dementia patients would not respond nor follow exercise instructions holding dumbbells, dowel, or theraband, instead place wrist weights on and instruct in overhead ball catch (keep count), reaching and movements within UE functional planes.
- Nu-step
- Omnicycle

Documentation:

Ther Act: 97530

1. Patient performed functional mobility in the hallway on the unit with HHA, no AD to access marked room door with moderate verbal cues identifying 1/3 trials.

Self-Care: 97535

2. Patient instructed in donning/doffing t-shirt with demonstration and 50% HOH assist to initiate proper sequencing with 50%verbal cues, Min A provided during return demonstration.

Case Study 3: Lopez, Patrick
Congestive Heart Failure (CHF)

Brief Review:

CHF is a chronic condition in which the heart does not pump blood as well as it should and fluid backs up into the lungs and the body. During diastolic, the heart can't fill sufficiently and during systolic, the heart doesn't pump out blood sufficiently. Narrow arteries and high blood pressure gradually leave the heart weak or stiff to fill and pump blood efficiently. Usually, CHF can be controlled with diet, medications, and rest. Diuretics are often used to decrease edema.

Some symptoms to look for:

- Shortness of breath (SOB)
- Fatigue
- Swollen lower extremities
- Rapid heartbeat
- Dry cough
- Water retention
- Excess urination
- Weight gain

Patient Profile:

<u>History/Complexities:</u>
Mr. Lopez age 79 y/o male admitted presenting with hx of present illness s/p hospitalization secondary to fluid overload and acute, yet chronic CHF exacerbation. The patient sustained a fall at home, sent to ER with SOB. Patient also has cellulitis of bilateral LE's.

Precautions: HTN, obesity, cardiac, fall, 2L continuous O2 via NC

Prior level of function (PLOF):

Patient lives with his wife in a single level house with 5 STE with bilateral handrails. Patient was modified independent with functional mobility using RW within the house and was gait training with SPC with home PT. Patient reported being independent with ADLs and Mod (I) for LB dressing using reacher. Patient sponge bathes himself sitting in front of his bathroom sink. Patient receives home health aide 3 days a week, 4 hours a day for shower assistance and IADLs. Patient owns a RW, SPC, tub bench and 3:1commode.

Assessment & Underlying impairment:

- Follows multi-step directions
- Safety awareness intact
- Oriented to person, place, and time
- 2+ pitting edema of bilateral LE's
- Static standing balance poor +, dynamic standing balance poor
- Functional transfers Max Ax2, bed mobility Max A, toileting Max Ax2, LB dressing TD, UB dressing CGA/Min A, self-feeding (I), functional mobility Max Ax2, hygiene/grooming (I).

Skilled justification:

Patient requires skilled OT services to facilitate independence with ADLs, develop and instruct in compensatory strategies, assess safety with AE, decrease edema in extremities, increase overall strength, improve activity tolerance, mobility, and transfers in order to enhance patient's QOL to be able to return to PLOF.

Mr. Lopez's goals

Short term:

1. Patient will increase static standing balance during ADLs to fair- w/o LOB and signs/symptoms of inadequate cardiac functioning in order to safely participate in activities of choice.
2. Patient will increase activity tolerance w/o signs of SOB and fatigue for 10 minutes during activities of choice and ADLs implementing 80% carryover of energy conservation techniques.
3. Patient will safely and efficiently perform LB dressing with Max A using a reacher with Min verbal cues to ensure safety in order to facilitate independence.

Long term:

1. Patient will safely and efficiently perform LB dressing with a reacher to achieve modified independence in order to return to PLOF.
2. Patient will increase activity tolerance w/o signs of SOB and fatigue to 30 minutes during activities of choice and ADLs implementing 100% carryover of energy conservation techniques.

Treatment interventions & Tips:

Activity tolerance & Strengthening

1. Have patient use Omnicycle Elite machine or nu-step. It is great for neurological, orthopedic, and cardiopulmonary rehabilitation.
2. Instead of focusing on strength training using repetition and weights, time exercise using weights. For example, 30 seconds of elbow flexion/extension followed by deep

breathing times 3 sets. This will promote activity tolerance training as well as strength training.

3. Catch/retrieve activities to self or to another person timed, grade accordingly.
4. Timed tabletop standing activities.
5. Instruct in E/C and work simplification techniques.

Edema Management

1. Instructed patient on edema management with the importance of LE's elevation above heart level to decrease edema and gentle retrograde massage towards lymph nodes to support drainage. *Please note some contraindications with retrograde massage technique must achieve service competency or reach advanced training before implementing this technique with a CHF patient.
2. Compression garments, only with MD order.
3. F/u with nursing if the patient is on diuretic "water pill" if not, ask for a reason.
4. Use a tape measure to monitor LE edema reduction if needed for braces etc. (Physical Therapy will usually monitor this in an SNF setting)
5. Instruct patient in bed rolling and side lying for pressure distribution using pillows.

ADLs

1. Instructed in AE for LB dressing (reacher, dressing stick, sock aide,LHS, shoe horn). Use theraband to simulate dressing training.
2. Educate patient on elastic laces, cutting sides of socks for better fit and reduction of tightness around ankles.
3. Instruct patient in pursed-lip breathing and work simplification techniques such as planning what to wear, what items needed, and where items are located a day before in order to to decrease risk of fatigue.

4. Commode and shower tub bench training as appropriate.
5. Educate patient on the importance of loose fitting clothing.
6. Use parallel bars or hallway rail for static standing or standing frame due to poor + balance as appropriate.

Documentation:

Ther Act: 97530

1. Patient instructed in proper bed positioning with the use of wedge/pillows for edema reduction for (B)LE's with good carryover of observed instructions. Pt instructed in supine to sit at EOB Mod/Max A + verbal cues, scooting and re-positioning self in bed Mod A + verbal cues and SPT from bed to w/c Mod Ax2 to ensure safety.

Ther-Ex: 97110

2. Patient utilized nu-step on resistance level 1 in order to increase strength, activity tolerance and ADL performance for 10-minutes, 30-45 seconds rest period incorporated during this activity, breathing emphasized.

Self-Care: 97535

3. Patient was instructed in LB dressing training using a reacher to thread legs through pant opening with moderate verbal and tactile cues for proper manipulation of AE and safety upon standing requiring, Max A to assume posture.

Testimonial 2: Michelle M. Savrann, MHA, OTR/L

QUINSIGAMOND Community College

Occupational Therapy Assistant
V: 508.854.4546 • F: 508.852.6943
www.qcc.edu

November 20, 2015

To whom it may concern,

It is a privilege to write this letter of recommendation on behalf of Timisha Daniels, an applicant to the Occupational Therapy Graduate Program. I have known Timisha since September 2010 when she began the Occupational Therapy Assistant Program at Quinsigamond Community College as her instructor and in my role as the Academic Fieldwork Coordinator. Since her graduation in 2012, Timisha has remained in contact with program faculty, to share her successes as an occupational therapy assistant, or to seek guidance in her pursuit of higher education in occupational therapy.

Timisha is an intelligent, motivated individual who possess remarkable self-awareness and capacity for self-advocacy. From the first class in the OTA program, Timisha demonstrated a level of passion and commitment for the occupational therapy profession and her education that went well beyond a first semester student. During her academic preparation, Timisha consistently prepared assignments that were of exceptional quality that reflected her curiosity, drive and commitment to her education and learning. While in the program Timisha frequently engaged in independent study and research, and regularly sought opportunities to discuss her interests and seek guidance. She has carried this trait into her work as a COTA. Timisha did not hesitate to ask thoughtful questions or provide comments reflect a degree of critical thinking and integration of material. Frequently her questions and comments enabled others to improve their comprehension of the subject matter and she quickly emerged as leader in the classroom, and easily gained the respect of her peers.

Timisha's attributes in the classroom were also displayed during her fieldwork experiences. Words used to describe Timisha during her fieldwork and reflected in her fieldwork evaluations include such comments as; "Timisha is a natural leader, always professional, has a great attitude, respectful and treats everyone with dignity, a team player, skilled at interacting with patients and families, flexible, adaptable, discreet when discussing clients, seeks help when needed and welcomes feedback" and "Timisha will be an asset wherever she goes". Her performance during her Fieldwork experience resulted in her receiving the Rose Capriolli Memorial Award for OTA student who consistently demonstrated excellence both in the classroom and clinical settings.

Timisha's performance in the OTA Program and her work as a COTA illustrate her passion for the profession, her motivation and drive for learning and her proclivity as a leader and advocate. At this juncture in her professional journey, I believe Timisha is an excellent capacity to benefit from the opportunity to advance her education in the field of occupational therapy.

If I can be of further assistance, please feel free to contact me.

Sincerely,

Michelle Savrann

Michelle M. Savrann, MHA, OTR/L
OTA Program Coordinator
Email: msavrann@qcc.mass.edu

670 West Boylston Street • Worcester, MA 01606 • www.QCC.edu

Case Study 4: Smith, Martha
Chronic Obstructive Pulmonary Disease (COPD)

Brief Review:

COPD is a term used broadly to describe a variety of pulmonary disorders such as chronic bronchitis, asthma, and emphysema. COPD is a common lung disease which makes it difficult to breathe. The walls of the alveoli lose their elasticity and the walls become thick then the air passage becomes plugged with mucus. During breathing, air is able to enter during inhalation, but unable to escape through exhalation because the air passage collapses, trapping stale air, leading to decreased gas exchange, increased carbon dioxide accumulation, hypoventilation, and stress on the heart. There is currently no cure.

Causes:
- Smoking
- Exposure to certain gases (pollution) and chemical fumes
- Family history
- Second-hand smoke

Signs & Symptoms:
- Dyspnea
- Wheezing
- Respiratory infection
- Trouble catching breath
- Chest tightness
- Fatigue
- Cough
- Cough up blood

Patient Profile:

History/ Complexities:
Mrs. Smith age 60 and gender female was sent out to the hospital from home secondary to increasing lethargy, cough, and SOB. Her admitting dx is pneumonia, acute exacerbation of chronic COPD. Pt uses O2 during the night time at home for the past few years. Pt is an active smoker with hx of depression, anxiety, CHF and HTN.

Precautions: falls, cardiac, 3L continuous O2 via NC

Prior level of function (PLOF):
Patient lives with her son in a 2-level townhouse. She resides on the first floor. The patient is independent with all ADLs and independent with functional mobility without AD. Pt is also independent in cooking, cleaning, and driving.

Assessment & Underlying impairment:

- Follows multi-step directions
- Safety awareness intact
- Oriented to person, place and time
- (B)UE WFL
- Static standing balance good-, dynamic standing balance fair
- Functional transfers CGA/Min A, bed mobility (S), toileting CGA/Min A, LB dressing Min A, UB dressing (I), self-feeding (I), functional mobility Min A, IADLs Mod A.

Skilled justification:
Patient requires skilled OT services to facilitate independence with ADLs, develop and instruct in compensatory strategies, assess safety with AE, increase strength, instruct in work simplification and energy conservation techniques, improve activity tolerance,

mobility and transfers in order to enhance patient's QOL to be able to return to prior level of living.

Mrs. Smith's goals

Short term goals:

1. Patient will safely and efficiently perform LB dressing supervised with use of AE as needed in order to facilitate independence and ensure safety with the implementation of E/C techniques.
2. Patient will increase activity tolerance w/o signs of SOB and fatigue during activities of choice, 5 minutes while maintaining >92% O2 saturation levels while implementing energy conservation techniques.
3. Patient will perform simple housekeeping task demonstrating adequate carryover and implementation of energy conservation techniques requiring CGA.

Long Term goals:

1. Patient will safely and efficiently perform LB dressing independently with the use of AE as needed with the implementation of E/C techniques to return to prior level of functioning.
2. Patient will perform housekeeping tasks independently with adequate carryover and implementation of energy conservation techniques.

Treatment interventions & Tips:

1. Have patient use Omnicycle Elite machine or Nu-step. Start with no resistance for 1-5 minute intervals, depending on patient's activity level.
2. Provide and review E/C and work simplification packet, followed by a verbal quiz to facilitate carryover.

3. Instruct in pursed-lip breathing to maintain safe O2 saturation levels.
4. Instruct patient in activity pacing and activity analysis for day-to-day task planning, such as organizing clothes for next day wear, placing pots/pans at a reasonable height that are used regularly, and hanging clothes in the closet.
5. Stress management training: Instruct in stop and breath technique with focused counting from 1-10 when feeling panicked due to difficulty in catching breathe.
6. Use AE for LB dressing (sock aide, reacher, shoe horn, long handle sponge, elastic laces) as needed or cross leg technique (have the patient bring one leg over the other versus bending over).
7. Create a task checklist for the patient to complete such as folding clothes, washing dishes/dry or placing items into overhead cabinets while being timed in order to have measurable data to assess improvement. You can also monitor how many rest breaks is required during an activity.

Documentation:

Ther-Ex: 97110

1. Patient utilized Nu-step machine, interval training on low resistance for 2-minutes of activity, 1-minute rest progressing to 5-minute activity for a total of 15 minutes, breathing, and upright sitting posture emphasized in order to improve activity tolerance and QOL.

Ther Act: 97530

2. Patient participated in light dishwashing task, standing at the kitchen sink with w/c behind and RW position in front requiring CGA to ensure safety while maintaining 95% O2

saturation level on 2L of O2 via NC x 2 seated rest periods within an 8-minute period.

Self-Care: 97535

3. Patient performed LB dressing (donning pants, socks, and slippers) implementing cross leg technique and deep breathing w/o use of AE (S) with minimal verbal cues for posture and task pacing.

Chapter 2
Case Study 5: Goldstein, Mark
Bilateral Knee Amputation

Brief Review:

Amputations can occur through trauma, birth defects, disease, and illness. Two broad categories that will often be seen in rehab is congenital amputation which is the absence of a limb at birth due to a birth defect and acquired amputation which is the loss of a limb due to trauma or surgery. Transfemoral amputation is known as AKA, above knee amputation. Transtibial amputation is known as BKA, below knee amputation. It tends to be rare to see a complete limb removal. It is important for therapists to be aware of the psychological adjustments that occur after amputation such as grieving, denial, anger, depression, and acceptance.

Causes:

- Diabetes
- Peripheral vascular disease (PVD)
- Motor vehicle accident
- Work-related injuries
- Tumors
- Burns
- Electrical injuries
- Birth defect
- Military combat

Post-operative care and intervention:

1. Decrease edema- Compression garment
2. Residual limb care/skin hygiene- Use a hand-held mirror, train patient on how to inspect skin, looking for normal healing vs abnormalities.
3. Decrease phantom pain
   a) massage residual limb
   b) use a shrinker
   c) reposition residual limb by propping on a pillow or cushion
   d) mirror box therapy
   e) TENs
   f) imagery biofeedback
4. Support wound healing
5. Residual limb wrapping per MD order
   Steps of wrapping (BKA):
   1. Bandage right below the knee
   2. Wrap in figure 8 pattern, inside to outside to prevent creasing
   3. Move up the leg, wrap above the knee
   4. Make 1-2 wraps above the kneecap, then bandage below knee again
   5. Tap or tie bandage in place, do not use pins
6. Increase proprioceptive input-massage, brushing, and deep pressure.
7. Instruct in ROM and strength training exercises.
8. Instruct in wear of shrinker or elastic bandage.
9. Cleanse of gel liner and wear
10. Prosthetic training
11. ADL/IADL training
12. Community reintegration
13. Patient and family education
14. Strength training

Patient Profile:

History/ Complexities:
Mr. Goldstein age 45 and gender male presented with bilateral BKA and uncontrolled DM. Patient was admitted for wound healing and prosthetic training due to loss of ADL function.

Precautions: falls

Prior level of function (PLOF):
Patient lives in an apartment with his son and was independent with ADL/IADLs prior to amputation surgery due to uncontrolled diabetes and lack of blood flow to lower extremities.

Assessment & Underlying impairment:

- Follows multi-step directions
- Safety awareness intact
- Oriented to person, place, and time
- (B)UE ROM WNL
- (B)UE MMT strength 3+/5
- Static standing balance unable, static sitting balance poor+
- Functional transfers Max A, bed mobility Max A, toileting TD, LB dressing Max A, UB dressing (I), self-feeding (I), functional mobility unable @ this time until prosthesis provided.

Skilled justification:
Patient requires skilled OT services to facilitate independence with ADLs, develop, and instruct in compensatory strategies, assess safety with AE, increase strength, modify environmental barriers, assess need for home modification, instruct in work simplification and energy conservation techniques, improve activity tolerance,

mobility and transfers in order to enhance patient's QOL to be able to return to their prior level of living.

Mr. Goldstein goals

Short term goals:

1. Patient will increase (B)UE to 4/5 strength to facilitate compensatory techniques in preparation for prosthesis training.
2. Patient will increase static sitting balance during ADLs to fair- in order to safely position and reposition self w/o LOB displaying good righting reactions to manage ADLs.
3. Patient will donn/doff LE garments (shorts, shrinker, gel liner, prosthetic) with Min A in order to achieve independence with ADLs.
4. Patient will safely propel w/c 100ft in hallway supervised with 20% verbal cues to support locomotion within his environment.

Long Term goals:

1. Patient will increase (B)UE to 5/5 strength to support compensatory techniques and prosthetic management to facilitate independence in ADLs.
2. Patient will increase static sitting balance during ADL to good in order to safely position and reposition self with good righting reactions to prevent LOB during ADL management and functional transfers.

Treatment interventions & Tips:

(B)UE Strengthening

1. In order to improve core muscles, instruct in abdominal crunches 10-15 reps x 3-4 sets.

2. In order to improve core muscles, have patient hold the center of a rolled-up sheet to pull self up and lower back down to the bed while the therapist holds the end of the sheet (modified sit-ups), grade activity accordingly.
3. Instruct in deep breathing.
4. Instruct in w/c push-ups to improve UE strength, triceps strengthening.
5. Use pullies, dumbbells. or dowel for strengthening.

Core Strengthening & Dynamic sitting balance

1. Seated on a therapy mat, have the patient perform lateral and forward trunk flexion while stacking cones.
2. Ball toss seated at the edge of the mat.

ADLs

1. Instruct in commode transfer board training .
3. Instruct patient in keeping good hygiene and care of residual limb, change shrinker socks more than once a day due to perspiration. (Antiperspirant CertainDri or a sprinkle of baking soda can be used on healed residual limbs, however, consult MD or prosthetist first).
4. Instruct patient in residual limb examination using a hand mirror.
5. Educate patient on the use of shrinker socks thickness or "ply", starting at 1-ply to 6-ply.
6. Instruct patient in shrinker sock care, daily night time wash with antibacterial soap and water or rubbing alcohol, followed by a wet towel to remove traces of rubbing alcohol.

Documentation:

W/c mgt: 97542

Patient was instructed in safe w/c propulsion in the hallway, mobilizing through doorways, around corners, maneuvering in small spaces (S) with min vc's for turns and locking/unlocking brakes, 50 ft. at a time tolerated to facilitate engagement in his environment.

Ther-Ex: 97110

Patient completed 15 reps x 3 sets of elbow flexion/ext., shoulder flexion/ext., and triceps flexion/ext. in order to increase overall functional performance and strength, breathing emphasized, rest periods incorporated as needed.

Self-Care: 97535

Patient performed LB dressing (donning pants) seated at EOB w/o the use of AE (S) with minimal verbal cues for side to side weight shifting in order to hike garment over waist, posture, and task pacing.

Case Study 4: Peters, Michael
Lymphedema

Brief Review:

Lymphedema is blockage of the lymphatic vessels leading to fluid retention. The build-up and swelling is often seen in the arms and legs resulting in pain and discomfort. It is easy to remember the meaning by simply separating the word, lymph for lymph nodes and edema for swelling. Once put together, swelling of lymph nodes. Lymphedema can be present at birth or from trauma such as burns, radiation, lymph compression from overweight and infections.

Signs & Symptoms:

- Burning & tingling pain
- Warm & redness
- Decreased flexibility of joints
- Heaviness of limbs
- Skin tightness
- Achy & pain at affected extremity
- Fever & Chill

Patient Profile:

<u>History/ Complexities:</u>
Mr. Peters age 70 and gender male, presents with fluid overload in both lower extremities. Patient sustained a fall at home at night when heading to the bathroom, unable to get up from the floor, patient's wife called the ambulance. Mr. Peters admitting dx is SOB and cellulitis of BLE's. Patient is obese, hx of MRSA of nares, endocarditis, and HTN. Patient does not use oxygen at home.
<u>Precautions:</u> falls, cardiac, 2L continuous O2 via NC

Prior level of function (PLOF):

Patient lives with his wife in a single level house with 5 STE and bilateral handrails. Patient was independent with functional mobility with RW within the house and was gait training with SPC with home PT. The patient was reported being independent with ADLs except LB dressing, requiring Min A for socks and shoes. Patient would bathe himself seated at the bathroom sink; patient owns a 3:1 commode.

Assessment & Underlying impairment:

- Follows multi-step directions
- Safety awareness intact
- Oriented to person, place and time
- (B)UE WFL
- Static standing balance poor, dynamic standing balance unable
- Functional transfers: Hoyer lift, bed mobility Max A, toileting TD, LB dressing TD, UB dressing Min A, UB bathing Min/Mod A, LB bathing TD, self-feeding (I), functional mobility TD.

Skilled justification:

Patient requires skilled OT services to facilitate independence with ADLs, develop and instruct in compensatory strategies, assess safety, AE training and management, increase strength, instruct in work simplification and energy conservation techniques, improve activity tolerance, mobility and transfers in order to enhance patient's QOL to be able to return to prior level of living.

Mr. Peters's goals

Short term goals:

1. Patient will increase the ability to safely propel self in wheelchair in the room/hallway with Min A, 50 feet, 25% verbal and tactile cueing in order to support mobility in one's environment safely until PLOF with mobility using RW achieved.
2. Patient will perform functional mobility with RW from bedroom to bathroom safely with Mod A and moderate verbal cues.
3. Patient will safely perform LB dressing with Max A using AE in order to facilitate independence with ADLs.
4. Patient will perform functional transfer from bed to w/c using a sliding board with Mod Ax2 and minimal verbal cues.

Long Term goals:

1. Patient will safely and efficiently perform LB dressing using appropriate AE with Min A in order to return to prior level of functioning.
2. Patient will perform functional mobility using RW from bedroom to bathroom safely, modify independent in order to return to a least restrictive environment.

Treatment interventions & Tips:

1. Instruct patient trained in the use of a leg lifter, if one is not available use a long bed sheet rolled and have patient crisscross anteriorly and posteriorly over lower leg to create support during movement.
2. Provide and review E/C and work simplification packet, followed by a verbal quiz to facilitate carryover and adopt better habits.

3. Instruct patient in edema management, using a wedge under BLE's and pumping ankles, *remember legs must be above the heart.
4. Instruct in pursed-lip breathing to maintain safe O2 saturation levels.
5. Have patient sit on therapy mat or EOB, wrap bed sheet across back, hold opposite ends and instruct patient in forward rocking motion to facilitate tactile feedback through feet, engage core, and promote sit to stand performance.
6. Make a small cut along the sides of the patient's socks to ease glide due to edema, thereafter instruct in donning/doffing using sock aide.
7. Provide patient with elastic laces for shoe management due to difficulty reaching LE's.
8. Instruct in w/c propulsion using brake extenders as needed.
9. Instruct in sliding board placement, posture control, and hand/feet placement during functional transfers using a beasy board or standard sliding board.
10. Instruct patient and nursing regarding a 2-hrs toileting schedule due to diuretic medication.
11. Educate patient on pitting edema and LE's weeping as fluid reduces.
12. Pt should use loose fitting clothes with instruction in LBD (theraband simulation) secondary swollen LE's.

Documentation:

W/C Mgt Training: 97542

1. Patient participated in w/c propulsion training in the hallway. Patient demonstrated competence to self-propel using (B)UE/LE's including turns, reversing and negotiating obstacles in his path for 25ft upon rest period with CS

+ 10% verbal cues to ensure safety. DNT with leg-rests on, patient also (I) with brake management.

Ther Act: 97530

2. Sit to supine Mod/Max A, scooting and repositioning self @ EOB Max Ax1. Patient was educated on safe and beneficial bed positioning using pillows/wedge in supine for (B)LE's edema reduction. Patient instructed in w/c<->bed SPT using bed rail for support during pivoting requiring Max Ax2 + verbal cues, thereafter patient instructed in bed to w/c transfer using the sliding board with verbal instruction on proper hand/feet placement to ensure safety during glide requiring Mod Ax2 + verbal cues.

Self-Care: 97535

3. Patient performed LB dressing (donning pants, socks, and slippers) using AE with Mod/Max A, mod vc's for deep breathing, posture, and task pacing in order to facilitate (I).

Testimonial #3

Dec. 4, 2016

After being hospitalized for a few weeks I was transferred to Green Hill in West Orange, NJ for rehabilitation. My therapist is Timisha Daniels (Tross) better known as "T". I was okay with going for therapy because I knew I needed it. However, after the first session, at that moment, I realized that this is not easy; and it hurt because your body is resisting and your muscles are screaming. All l wanted to do was to go home.

Ms. T started at the first session focused on calming me down. Between exercises we would talk about various subjects, we laughed at some silly things and a rapport actually started from that first session. This was very important to me and made me feel like I wasn't going through this alone.

A patient has enough medical issues; frustration with the inability to take care of self and to add feeling alone only creates more problems. Therapy is not easy and I wouldn't recommend it to any one (just kidding!). I realize now how important it is to improve physically and mentally. I was in bad shape physically and not much better mentally. I've never had physical and occupational therapy, now that I'm in PT/OT, great respect for the profession. Working with disabled patients is quite a challenge.

I'm making very good progress thanks to "T" my therapist and "T" my friend.

---Johanna Ostman

Case Study 7: Baker, Joan
Status-post total hip replacement (THR)

Brief Review:

What is a hip joint? The hip is a ball-and-socket joint that is formed between the thigh bone (femur) and the pelvis. This joint is a major weight-bearing joint that carries as much as three times our body weight. So what happens when a hip joint is replaced? The damaged bone and cartilage is removed (femoral head and acetabulum) and replaced with artificial parts called prostheses. This implant is a metal stem that is placed into the hollow center of the femur.

The muscles around the hip joint after a hip replacement is weak. How do you protect the hip?

- DO NOT bend past 90 degrees.
- DO NOT cross legs.
- DO NOT let the leg roll inward (internal rotation of hip aka pigeon toes).
- DO NOT let knees touch while sitting and lying down.

Signs of hip site infection

- Redness
- Warmth
- Increased drainage
- Foul smell
- Increased pain
- fever

Patient Profile:

History/Complexities:
Mrs. Baker age 75 and gender female, was admitted to hospital due to a left hip replacement secondary to a fall while shoveling snow. Patient has hx of HTN, A-fib, and asthma.

Precautions: falls, WBAT of (L) hip, hip precautions

Prior level of function (PLOF): Patient resides in private residence. Patient lives in a 2-story house and lives alone. Patient owns a chair lift and was independent with all ADLs. Patient uses an SPC for locomotion in and outside of home. Patient owns a 3:1 commode, shower grab bars, SPC and RW. Patient has close relatives, no children.

Assessment & Underlying impairment:

- Follows multi-step directions
- Safety awareness intact
- Oriented to person, place and time
- (B)UE WFL
- (B)UE strength impaired 4-/5
- Static standing balance fair, dynamic standing balance fair-
- Functional transfers: Min A, bed mobility Min A, toileting Min/Mod A, LB dressing Mod A, UB dressing (I), UB bathing (I), LB bathing Mod A, self-feeding (I), functional mobility with RW Min A.

Skilled justification:
Patient requires skilled OT services to facilitate independence with ADLs, develop and instruct in compensatory strategies, assess safety with AE, increase strength, instruct in work simplification and energy conservation techniques, improve activity tolerance,

mobility, and transfer in order to enhance patient's QOL to be able to return to prior level of living.

Mrs. Baker's goals

Short term goals:

1. Patient will increase (B)UE strength to 4/5 in order to increase independence with ADLs tasks.
2. Patient will perform all aspects of toileting using raised toilet seat or commode with Min A and minimal verbal cues to ensure safety.
3. Patient will safely perform all aspect of LB dressing with Min A using AE in order to facilitate independence with self-care.
4. Patient will sustain dynamic standing balance for 5 minutes in order to perform simple housekeeping tasks, implementing compensatory and E/C techniques with 100% carryover of safety strategies with fair balance.

Long Term goals:

1. Patient will safely perform all aspect of LB dressing Mod (I) using AE in order to facilitate independence with self-care.
2. Patient will sustain dynamic standing balance for 15 minutes in order to perform simple housekeeping tasks, implementing compensatory, and E/C techniques with 100% carryover of safety strategies with G- balance.

Treatment interventions & Tips:

1. Review, discuss and quiz hip precautions on the 1st tx session to promote hip precaution adherence.

2. Educate patient on proper positioning of (L) hip during rise/sit training with visual and verbal demonstration prior to return demonstration.
3. After 3rd tx session, introduce AE (hip kit), followed by training for proper management and manipulation. Provide patient with elastic laces.
4. If no elastic laces are available, cut very thin strips of theraband, wrap ends of theraband with duck tape or white tape (nurses will often have this in their carts). This will allow you to thread the band through sneaker holes and provide elasticity.
5. For patients living alone, educate them on the benefits of Lifeline.
6. Use baby powder to ease sock aide glide.
7. Assess and modify the use of towel on tub transfer bench to support slide and prevent shearing force.
8. Educate on TEDs to prevent DVT.
9. Instruct in safe car transfer, if no car is available simple use a hi-lo bedside table. Increase the table height to full capacity and place over the edge of therapy mat to simulate the roof of a car.
10. Instruct in tub transfer, if there's no tub available, use a hi-lo bedside table, increase height to the highest point and place it on the floor to simulate stepping in/out of a tub, focusing on clearing tub height.
11. Use flexible sock aide to facilitate slip sock or plastic bag TED stocking hike up leg. *TED hose will slide easily over plastic, don't forget to use a dressing stick or reacher to remove plastic bag once the hose is within arm's reach. Steps to donning compression stocking easily:
    1. Place plastic bag over feet
    2. Place stocking over bag, pull up leg
    3. Remove bag through compression stocking hole

Documentation:

Ther-ex: 97110

1. Patient instructed in (B)UE ther-ex using 2lbs dumbbell elbow flexion/ext. 15 reps x 3 sets, scapular retraction/protraction 15 reps x 3 sets, shoulder flexion/ext. 15 reps x 3 sets and modified w/c push-ups 10 reps x 3 sets with LLE extended forward in order to increase strength, activity tolerance and ADL performance, breathing emphasized and rest periods incorporated throughout strength training to prevent physical exertion. Pt provided with cold pack at L hip for pain management and edema control after ther-ex. Patient reported pain regression to 2/10 from 5/10 after pain modality applied at the end of session.

Neuro Re-ed: 97112

2. Patient was instructed in safe dynamic standing balance F with unilateral support from RW during tabletop activities reaching forward and laterally with focus on standing tolerance, sustained @ a time, 3 minutes. Patient also instructed in table wiping, moving items and placing it on the overhead shelf with CGA to ensure safety and balance.

Self-Care: 97535

3. Patient was seen in the room for morning ADLs training. Patient demo competence to move around in bed and transition from supine to sit with CGA + min verbal and tactile cueing for proper positioning of L hip. Patient performed UB dressing and sponge bathing (I), however, Min/Mod A was required for LB dressing and bathing using LHS and reacher to thread legs through pant opening. Pt required Min A to use sock aide appropriately and safely to donn socks. Patient utilized reacher to retrieve slippers off the floor from under bed w/o compromising hip precautions.

Ther Act: 97530

1. Patient recalled 2/3 hip precaution correctly. Patient was observed during supine to sit transition with bed semi-reclined, implementing proper hip precaution techniques CGA + minimal verbal cues. Bed to w/c SPT Min A with minimal verbal cues for proper hand/feet placement.

Testimonial 4: Carolyn Truncellito

"T" has helped me so very much since I came to occupational therapy. She has always encouraged me that I could do a little bit more, and I can! She challenged me as no others have. I couldn't get into bed by myself and now I can. Her positive thinking helps me so much. I couldn't sit and get up from a lower chair, but with T's encouragement, I can. Now, every time I try to do something, I think of a positive way, not negative, because of T. Just recently, I had trouble getting up from my rollator and she encouraged me to use my legs more and it worked. She doesn't baby me as some have. She challenges and expects a little bit more and most of all, positive thinking. "T" has meant so very much to my health and getting better. I am now mobile and independent.

--Carolyn Truncellito

Case Study 7: Markers, Dory
Lung Cancer

Brief Review:

Cancer (carcinoma) is an abnormal tissue growth that spreads or metastasizes throughout the body. The cancer type is diagnosed by the tissue from which it first developed. According to the Medical Dictionary, a tumor is a "swelling of a part of the body, generally without inflammation, caused by an abnormal growth of tissue, whether benign or malignant." Lung cancer can be detected by chest x-ray. There are different cancer stages. Cancer localized to one region may be classified as stage 1, cancer spread to an adjacent local region such as left breast to left axilla stage 2, and stage 3 disease spreads to another organ and lastly stage 4 is when the disease is widespread throughout the body affecting multiple systems and organs. Cancer treatment consists of radiation therapy, surgery, and chemotherapy.

Patient Profile:

History/ Complexities:
Mrs. Marker age 62 and gender female, was admitted to the hospital due to a complaint of SOB, chronic cough, and chest pain. Pt dx with stage 1 lung cancer and currently undergoing chemotherapy. Patient has been a cigarette smoker for 30 years and is still actively smoking. Pt has hx of HTN, depression, ETOH, and anxiety.

Precautions: generalized weakness, SOB, fatigue, 02@ 4L via NC, falls.

Prior level of function (PLOF):

Patient resides in an apartment complex on the first floor, elevator building. Patient has one son who occasionally comes to visit her, but he does not provide ADL support; only grocery shopping at times. Patient had 3 falls within 8 months at home and declines home care. Patient is eligible for oxygen at home but is non-compliant with use. Patient owns a RW, SPC and 3:1 commode. Patient was independent with ADLs and used local bus for community mobility.

Assessment & Underlying impairment:

- Follows multi-step directions
- Decreased safety awareness
- Oriented to person, place, and time
- (B)UE ROM WFL
- (B)UE strength impaired 3+/5
- Static standing balance fair+, dynamic standing balance fair
- Functional transfers: Min A, bed mobility Min A, toileting Min A, LB dressing Min/Mod A, UB dressing (S), UB bathing Min A, LB bathing Mod A, self-feeding (I), hygiene/grooming (S), functional mobility with RW Min A.

Skilled justification:

Patient requires skilled OT services to facilitate independence with ADLs, instruct in work simplification, develop and instruct in compensatory strategies, assess safety, and train in energy conservation techniques in order to improve QOL, increase strength, improve activity tolerance, mobility, ADLs, and functional transfers in order to be able to return to prior level of living.

Mrs. Markers's goals

Short term goals:

1. Patient will tolerate UE armbike seated for 3 minutes while maintaining O2 saturation levels >90% w/ one rest period incorporated in order to improve management of self-care tasks, strength, and activity tolerance.
2. Patient will be able to transition from supine position to sit at EOB using bedrail when needed with CGA + 25% verbal and tactile cues to ensure safety.
3. Patient will complete all aspects of morning hygiene care (comb hair, oral care, wash face) seated in w/c @ bathroom sink within 8 minutes, supervised.

Long Term goals:

1. Patient will tolerate UE armbike seated for 10 minutes while maintaining O2 saturation levels >90% w/o rest breaks in order to improve management of self-care tasks, strength and activity tolerance.
2. Patient will be able to transition from supine to sit at EOB independently.

Treatment intervention & Tips:

1. Provide guided imagery (meditation, visualization) to reduce stress, anxiety, pain, and depression.
2. Cryotherapy to shrink the tumor that is blocking airway and the pain, must achieve service competency before performing.
3. Modify tasks and environment: use AE for ADLs to decrease fatigue, educate patient on having a chair in every room due to limited activity tolerance to facilitate safety and decrease the risk of falls.

4. Educate and instruct in energy conservation techniques, follow 4 P's
    a. Planning
    b. Pacing
    c. Prioritizing
    d. Positioning
5. Provide advocacy and refer to support group during caregiver meetings.
6. Instruct in pursed-lip breathing.
7. Provide AE/AD such as shower chair for showers etc.
8. Support patient in static sitting balance @ EOB with focus on an erect posture with arms wide holding bed while breathing deeply, looking at patient's diaphragm to support respiration.
9. Do not use heavy weights until after chemo and radiation is complete, focus on isometric/AROM exercises, stretching and number of repetitions.
10. Educate patient on positioning in bed for optimal breathing, using pillows, wedge or elevating bed height.
11. Assess safety with rollator secondary limited activity tolerance.
12. Perform simulated activities such as grocery shopping (rollator basket as a cart) with a list, cleaning and meal preparation with verbal instructions on how to pace and organize.

Documentation:

Ther-ex: 97110

1. Patient utilized UE armbike seated with supplemental O2 via NC 3L for 5 minutes x 3 rest periods with no resistance, followed by guided breathing. Pt's O2 level ranged from 89% to 93% during this activity.

Ther Act: 97530

2. Patient instructed in safe supine to sit transition using bed-rail for added support and positioning techniques to prevent physical exertion, SOB, and dizziness upon rising, Min A + moderate verbal cues provided.

Chapter 3
Case Study 9: Stewart, Barbara (UTI, E-Coli & MRSA of nares)

Brief Review:

There will be times when a patient displays multiple complications affecting their recovery. In order to understand how to care for this patient, it is best to understand how UTI, E-Coli, and MRSA can affect overall functional performance.

UTI:
A urinary tract infection is an infection/bacteria of the urinary system which includes the kidneys, bladder, and urethra. A symptom of the bladder and urethra is pelvic pain, pain during urination and blood in urine. A symptom of the kidney is back pain, nausea, vomiting, and fever. Elderly people are prone to UTI due to diabetes, bowel and urinary incontinence, immobility, kidney stones, and urinary catheter just to name a few.

What to look for since symptoms may be different with seniors?

- Cramping
- Vaginal irritation
- Fatigue
- Fever
- Strong or foul-smelling urine
- Frequent & urgent need to urinate
- Complaint of pressure in the lower pelvis
- Confusion
- Behavioral changes
- Dark urine
- Cloudy urine
- Blood in urine

Patient's are usually placed on antibiotics to treat a UTI. When working with a patient that has a UTI, universal precautions must be adhered such as hand washing and using gloves and gowns during toileting or contact with bodily fluids.

E-Coli:

(Escherichia coli)

This is bacteria commonly found in the intestines, usually causes no harm, but a common way to acquire E-Coli is through contaminated food resulting in food poisoning. Other effects from E-coli is pneumonia, UTI, and breathing problems. It can cause abdominal cramps, vomiting, and bloody diarrhea.

MRSA of nares

(Methicillin-resistant Staphylococcus Aureus)

This is a bacteria contracted in the nose and on the skin. MRSA can be picked up in the hospital or community. It is considered a "superbug" according to Centers of Disease Control (CDC) due to its resistance of multiple antibiotics. Individuals who are at risk of MRSA infection are those with skin breaks, hospital patients with IV, burns, weak immune system, pneumonia etc. MRSA can be transmitted via droplets such as coughing. It is recommended to wear a mask when working with a patient who has MRSA of the nares in an isolated area (droplet precautions). Gloves and gowns are recommended for skin infection MRSA (contact precautions). MRSA is very contagious so patients are often placed on isolation until cleared by nursing.

Patient Profile:

History/ Complexities:
Mrs. Stewart is a 73-year-old female, admitted due to acute renal failure disease baseline secondary to UTI. Patient has a foley catheter due to urinary retention. Patient underwent hemoglobin transfusion. Patient was recently dx with CHF and placed on 2L of O2 via NC. Patient had a renal sonogram and renal scan which showed a decreased flow of the right kidney near nonfunctional, mildly atrophic right kidney with a small cyst within the midpole region. Patient has a history of superficial bladder CA in June 2016, UTI, anemia, and acute renal disease.

Precautions: droplet precautions, R arm PICC line, cardiac, O2 @ 2L via NC PRN, E-coli (+) urine contract precautions, foley catheter and MRSA of nares droplet precaution—In isolation per nursing

Prior level of function (PLOF):
Patient lives alone in an apartment on the 3rd floor with elevator, no stairs to enter inside and outside. Patient uses rollator and owns SPC. Patient is independent with all ADLs, however, receives assistance from daughter for shopping.
Assessment &Underlying impairment:

- Follows multi-step directions
- Safety awareness intact
- Oriented to person, place, and time
- (B)UE WFL
- Activity tolerance for ADLs/functional tasks 1-3 minutes
- Static standing balance good, dynamic standing balance fair+
- Functional transfers: CGA, bed mobility (S), toileting CGA/Min A, LB dressing Min A, UB dressing (I), UB bathing (I), LB bathing Min A, self-feeding (I), functional mobility with rollator CGA.

Skilled justification:
Patient requires skilled OT services to facilitate independence with ADLs, develop and instruct in compensatory strategies, assess safety and training in the proper management of AE, increase strength, instruct in work simplification and energy conservation techniques, improve activity tolerance, mobility and transfers in order to enhance patient's QOL to be able to return to prior level of living.

Mrs. Stewart's goals

Short term goals:

1. Patient will safely perform functional activities of choice for 5 minutes w/o signs/symptoms of physical exertion and inadequate cardiac output in order to return to prior level of functional performance.
2. Patient will demonstrate 70% accuracy with foley catheter management safely in order to facilitate independence and decrease caregiver assistance.
3. Patient will perform LB bathing using LHS supervised with 20% verbal cues for proper carryover of instructed techniques to prevent physical exertion in order to improve self-care management.

Long Term goals:

1. Patient will demonstrate 100% accuracy with foley catheter management safely in order to facilitate independence with perineal care.
2. Patient will perform LB bathing using LHS modified independently with good carryover of instructed techniques to prevent physical exertion in order to improve self-care management

Treatment intervention & Tips:

1. Provide, discuss, and review E/C and work simplification packets.
2. Be sure to follow universal precautions during catheter management training, (donning/doffing catheter, hygiene, and care).
3. Have patient perform bed making task while you time their activity for measurable documentation.
4. Instruct in pursed-lip breathing.
5. Any equipment patients use such as walker, weight, AE should be kept in the patient room until d/c or properly sanitized.
6. Instruct patient in activity organization by setting a timer, analyzing activities, and creating daily task completion list prior engagement.
7. Perform ADL training using reacher and LHS to support O2 saturation and prevention of over exertion.
8. Instruct in diaper management, peeling, and attaching sticky stripe while seated.

Documentation:

Self-Care: 97535

1. Patient was trained in emptying and cleaning catheter bag safely, instructions provided in set-up, hand placement in order to prevent drip, seal and cleanse with moderate verbal cues and 80% return demonstration.

Ther Act: 97530

2. Patient completed the bed making activity, tucking fitted bed sheet, spreading top sheet, placing pillows into a pillowcase and maneuvering around the bed with CGA x 1

LOB requiring righting reaction assistance. Patient completed the bed-making task in 11-minutes x 2 seated rest breaks, breathing emphasized, Spo2 on 2L of O2 via NC 94%.

Case Study 10: Butler Sr., Bob
Parkinson Disease

Brief Review:

Parkinson Disease (PD) also known as Shaking Palsy is a slow chronic progressive disease that affects the nervous system resulting in four cardinal signs: resting tremors, rigidity, bradykinesia and postural instability. The cause of PD is unknown; however, the current research shows that low or failing dopamine levels contribute to PD. In other words, certain nerve cells in the brain called dopamine, which is a chemical messenger, breaks down or die. The symptom complex of PD is called Parkinsonism, not all patients with parkinsonism have PD. There are 5 stages of PD which at end-stage results in confinement to a bed or w/c requiring total assistance.

Signs & Symptoms:

- Shuffling gait
- Decreased motor control
- Bradykinesia (moving extremely slow)
- Resting tremors
- Stiff and painful joints
- Loss of fine/gross motor
- Mask-like face
- Monotone voice
- Muscle Fatigue
- Dysphagia
- Memory Loss
- Retropulsion

Patient Profile:

History/Complexities:
Mr. Butler age 53 and gender male, presents a 4-year history of PD and was admitted d/t fall in the kitchen. Patient's wife reports he has been a little more unsteady within the last month with increased drooling, c/o muscle fatigue and tremors. Patient has hx of depression, HTN, and CHD. Pt has R foot drop and currently wears AFO.

Precautions: falls, cardiac, R foot drop

Prior level of function (PLOF):
Mr. Butler is married with 2 adult children who live close by with 2 STE house. Mr. Butler was Mod (I) for self-feeding, (S) for hygiene/grooming and (S) for UBD. His wife provides Min A for LB dressing and toileting. He is Mod (I) for ambulation with an RW. Mr. Butler's wife does the cooking, cleaning, laundry, and shopping. Mr. Butler had completed home PT 1 week prior to the fall in the kitchen reaching for an item in his cabinet. Mrs. Butler is available to provide 24 hours care with assistance from their children.

Assessment & Underlying impairment:

- Follows two-step directions
- Safety awareness decreased
- Oriented to person, place and time
- (L)UE ROM of shoulder impaired, 6/10 pain
- Static standing balance fair -, dynamic standing balance poor +
- Stand tolerance <1 minute
- Functional transfers: Mod A, bed mobility Mod A, toileting Mod A, LB dressing Mod/Max A UB dressing Min A,

UB bathing Min A, LB bathing Mod A, self-feeding Min A, functional mobility Mod A.

Skilled justification:

Skilled OT services are warranted to maximize (I) w/ADLs, develop, and instruct in compensatory strategies, adaptation techniques, assess the need for AE/AD, maximize rehab potential, increase safety awareness, develop and instruct in exercise program, improve functional transfers, mobility and activity tolerance to facilitate independence with ADLs in order to enhance patient's QOL to be able to return to prior level of living.

Mr. Butler's goals

Short term goals:

1. Patient will increase (L)UE ROM to 0-90 degrees' shoulder flexion w/ 3/10 pain in order to perform UB dressing, hygiene, and hair care.
2. Patient will increase supported stand tolerance to 2 minutes during functional task w/o LOB and/or signs of physical exertion, CGA/Min A.
3. Patient will safely perform self-feeding using appropriate AE (S) with s/u in order to decrease spillage and facilitate PLOF.
4. Patient will increase dynamic standing balance when reaching outside BOS to Fair demonstrating good understanding of righting reaction techniques, stabilization and compensatory strategies in order to reduce the risk of falls.

Long Term goals:

1. Patient will increase (L)UE ROM to a functional level of 0-120 degrees' shoulder flexion, absent pain in order to perform UB dressing, hygiene and hair care.

2. Patient will demonstrate competence to maintain supported stand tolerance for 10 minutes during functional tasks w/o LOB and/or signs of physical exertion, supervised.

Treatment intervention & Tips:

1. Assess & provide weighted utensils.
2. Assess & provide rocker knives, scoop dishes, long straws, electric razor, and cups with lids as appropriate.
3. Educate patient on home modification/adaptation such as stair lift and throw rugs removal.
4. Female: front fastener bras (velcro closures) or sports bra, unisex: button hooks.
5. Assess & provide AE as appropriate (elastic lace, LHS, reacher sock aide etc.).
6. Focus on flexors stretch (hip, knee, elbow, hamstrings) during dynamic sitting and core strengthening activities.
7. Add fluorescent tape on the floor as a point of reference during functional mobility for stride length & step strategies.
8. Have patient verbalize step-by-step activities to decrease "freezing". For example: when walking, have the patient say, "take bigger steps".
9. Perform activities in front of a mirror for visual feedback.
10. Dynamic bending training reaching for cones on the floor while seated.
11. Use omnicycle/bike for fluidity of motion.
12. Rhythmic music or beats to decrease freezing (can be helpful in most cases).
13. Instruct patient in weight shifting and trunk rotation during reaching tasks.
14. Put hula-hoop on the floor or use tape to create a circle and have patient mobilize around it in order to improve pivoting.

15. Incorporate medium to large physio-ball for core training, postural awareness and stabilization on therapy mat placing in front for trunk flexion or behind.
16. Use moist heat prior to ROM exercise to decrease pain and increase movement.

Documentation:

Ther-Ex: 97110

1. Patient provided with MHP prior to gentle PROM of left GH joint in supine in all functional planes 10 reps x 3 sets in order to decrease pain level and increase shoulder ROM to facilitate ADL management, rest periods incorporated as needed.

Self-Care: 97535

2. Pt provided with weighted spoon and scoop dish during breakfast for self-feeding training. Pt required s/u of meal, opening of milk cartoon and removal of straw paper. Pt was instructed in dynamic tripod grasp using (R) hand to scoop food towards the higher end of the scoop dish in order to bring food to mouth with minimal spillage CGA/Min A + 50% verbal cues.

Case Study 11: Jackson, Martha
Right hand contracture (spastic clenched fist)

Brief Review:

A contracture is a deformity that results in stiffness and constriction in the connective tissue in the body which can occur in muscles, tendons, skin, bone, and ligaments. When the connective tissue becomes less flexible, it restricts normal movement. A muscular contracture is the shortening and tightening of muscles often seen with stroke patients. A joint contracture is in the joint capsule where two bones meet which is often seen with osteoarthritis and rheumatoid arthritis patients. Skin contracture is scarring, often seen with burn victims.

Patients prone for contractures:

- Stroke patients
- Osteoarthritis patients
- Rheumatoid patients
- Cerebral palsy patients
- Muscular dystrophy patients
- Polio patients
- Multiple Sclerosis patients
- Parkinson Disease patients
- Dementia patients
- Patient's in bed for an extended period of time
- TBI patients etc.

Patient Profile:

History/ Complexities:
Mrs. Jackson 79 y/o gender female is a resident of John Doe LTC facility and present with hx of OA, referred to skilled OT services for contracture management and generalized muscle weakness secondary to left MCP joint ulnar drift and spastic clenched fist of right hand causing poor hygiene and pain during manipulation. Patient will benefit from skilled OT services for orthotic management and training to improve pain, skin integrity, and ROM.

Precautions: pain

Prior level of function (PLOF):
Patient resides as a resident of this John Doe LTC facility.Bed mobility Mod A, Self-feeding Min A, Hygiene/grooming Min/Mod A, Toileting Mod A, UB dressing Min A, LB dressing Max A

Assessment & Underlying impairment:

- Follows multi-step directions
- Fine motor coordination: impaired
- Oriented to person, place, and time
- (L) hand MCP 3/10 pain, (R) 2, 3, 4, 5 digits 6/10 pain during movement
- Bilateral shoulders WFL
- CLOF: Bed mobility Max A, Self-feeding Max A, Hygiene/grooming Mod/Max A, Toileting Mod/Max A, UB dressing Mod A, LB dressing Max A

Skilled justification:
Skilled OT services are warranted to improve QOL w/ADLs, develop and instruct in compensatory strategies, adaptation techniques, assess the need for AE/AD, maximize rehab potential, increase safety awareness, develop and instruct in exercise program,

provide caregiver and patient training on orthotic management and hygiene in order to enhance patient's functional abilities with the least amount of pain.

Mrs. Jackson's goals

Short term goals:

1. Patient will be able to tolerate PROM of left hand MCP joint to reduce tightness and decrease pain to 0/10 for splint training.
2. Patient will be able to tolerate PROM of the right hand (2,3,4,5 fingers) to reduce tightness and decrease pain to 3/10 in order to tolerate palmar guard to maintain skin integrity.
3. Patient will tolerate left deviation hand splint with finger separators for up to 4 hours w/ minimal signs of redness, swelling, discomfort or pain.
4. Patient will perform self-feeding utilizing universal cuff utensil holder on (L) hand in order to scoop and bring food to mouth with minimal spillage, Mod A with s/u.

Long Term goals:

1. Patient will tolerate left deviation resting hand splint with finger separators worn at night for up to 8 hours w/ no signs of redness, swelling, discomfort or pain.
2. Patient will perform self-feeding utilizing universal cuff utensil on (L) hand in order to scoop and bring food to mouth, Min A with s/u to achieve PLOF.

Treatment intervention & Tips:

Left MCP ulnar deviation

1. Place hand flat on a table, support wrist, have the patient perform finger (spreads) add/abduction
2. Place tape vertically on the table with patient's hand flat on the table; have patient move wrist lateral towards the target with tactile cues.
3. Instruct patient to lift finger (one finger at a time) with hand flat on the table.
4. Joint mobilization (gliding technique of carpal bones)
5. E-stim (Neuro-Re-Ed) for spasticity reduction
6. Moist heat followed by prolonged stretch
7. Finger Opposition exercise, may need to grade this activity
8. Utilize theraputty for in-hand manipulation

Clenched spastic right hand

1. Use a damp hand towel to cleanse creases between fingers and palms.
2. Gentle PROM
3. Due to high sensitivity to touch and movement, dip hand in warm water followed by prolonged stretch.
4. Ultrasound (3 MHz) applied to wrist flexors for tendon release to improve splint wear and/or ROM training.
5. Ultrasound in water, decrease pain
6. E-stim (Neuro-Re-Ed) for spasticity reduction

Documentation:

Ther-Ex: 97110

Patient was provided with MHP for b/l hands prior to gentle PROM of fingers with a prolonged stretch 10 reps x 3 sets with emphasis on finger and wrist extension to decrease tightness/

contracture for self-feeding and clothing management. Patient verbalized pain reduction of 5/10.

Self-Care: 97535

Patient was seen in the morning for self-feeding management. Pt was instructed in managing items of food tray implementing compensatory techniques. Pt was provided with CGA during cup lid removal using (L)UE, Mod A for milk carton, sugar packets Max A, and placement of straw in milk cartoon after pouring milk into cereal Min A. Patient maintained a grasp of small milk carton during pouring with minimal spillage. Pt utilized universal cuff on (L) hand to scoop cereal to bring to mouth Min A + verbal cues.

Orthotic Training: 97760

Patient tolerated left deviation resting hand splint with finger separators for 2hrs w/o signs of redness, swelling, discomfort, or pain in order to facilitate normal anatomical position and skin integrity. Pt was educated on wear schedule, assessed fitting, and performed skin checks before, during, and after application.

Case Study 12: Flynn, Bob
Coronary Artery Bypass Graft

Brief Review:

Coronary Artery Bypass Graft: Abbreviated CABG. CABG is a bypass surgery that creates new routes or repairs blocked or clogged coronary arteries. This bypass allows oxygen and nutrients to flow to the heart muscles. An artery is taken from the chest or leg for grafting. Once a patient has this type of surgery where a cardiac surgeon makes an incision down the middle of the chest then saws through the sternum resulting in sternal precautions and a strict cardiac regiment/precaution. Sternal precautions are usually up to 8 weeks after surgery or longer depending on surgeon's orders.

Cardiac & Sternal Precautions:

- NO hyperextension of shoulders
- NO prolonged overhead activity
- Avoid hot temperatures (hot showers, tubs)
- NO driving
- DO not lift anything over 10lbs
- DO not push or pull forcefully with your arms
- Do not reach behind you
- DO not push with your arms to stand up, use legs with assistance as needed
- Always use a pillow when coughing or sneezing

Patient Profile:

History/Complexities:
Mr. Flynn age 57 and gender male, sustained a fall at home but was able to get up from the floor, however, the next day, the patient went to the hospital due to a complaint of SOB, angina, and dizziness. Patient underwent a cardiac catheterization. He had a positive nuclear stress test that showed reduced blood flow to the left ventricle. Pt had a CABG surgery. Patient referred to skilled OT services for cardiac rehabilitation. Pt has hx of high cholesterol, HTN, drug abuse for COC 10 years sober.

Precautions: sternal precautions, cardiac precautions

Prior level of function (PLOF):
Patient resides in an apartment complex on the second floor with 12 STE once inside the building, 5 steps to negotiate outside the building. Patient was independent with all ADLs and ambulated w/o AD. Patient drives to the supermarket to get groceries and laundry mat to wash clothes. Patient has a girlfriend, but no children. Patient does not own adaptive equipment.

Assessment & Underlying impairment:

- Follows multi-step directions
- Oriented to person, place and time
- (B)UE strength impaired 3+/5
- Static standing balance good-, dynamic standing balance fair+
- Functional transfers: Min A, bed mobility Mod A, toileting Mod A, LB dressing Mod A, UB dressing Mod A, self-feeding (I), hygiene/grooming Min A, sit to stand Min A, functional mobility with HHA, Min A.

Skilled justification:

Patient requires skilled OT services to facilitate independence with ADLs, develop and instruct in compensatory strategies, assess safety, implement energy conservation techniques in order to improve QOL, increase strength, instruct in work simplification, improve activity tolerance, mobility, ADLs and functional transfers in order to be able to return to prior level of living.

Mr. Flynn's goals

Short term goals:

1. Patient will utilize omnicycle (cardiac mode) for 15 minutes seated with activity performance >70% in order to increase endurance, improve management of self-care tasks, and strength.
2. Patient will safely perform UB dressing Min A with minimal verbal and tactile cueing, implementing compensatory techniques and maintaining sternal precaution.
3. Patient will safely and efficiently perform LB dressing with Min A using AE as appropriate in order to perform basic ADL tasks with increased (I) and safety.
4. Patient will safely perform functional activities of choice while standing for 3 minutes w/o signs/symptoms of physical exertion, inadequate cardiac input/output, and SOB in order to return to prior level of skill performance.
5. Patient will safely and efficiently perform light housekeeping tasks with Min A while maintaining good balance and displaying good safety awareness with the implementation of energy conservation techniques.

Long Term goals:

1. Patient will utilize omnicycle (cardiac mode) for 15 minutes seated with activity performance >90% in order to

increase endurance, improve management of self-care tasks and strength.

2. Patient will safely and efficiently perform light housekeeping tasks independently while maintaining normal balance and displaying good safety awareness with the implementation of energy conservation techniques.

Treatment intervention & Tips:

1. Perform UB dressing by keeping arms in front and reaching across the body to pull shirt around back and neck.
2. Perform semi-sit to stand training to increase quad strength to compensate for rise/sit performance.
3. Bend with knees and push with legs to roll onto the side, move legs off the bed, hang over the bed while maintaining side lying position then push legs against the bed and using abdominal muscles in the transition from supine to sit.
4. Donning jackets use flip over head technique.
5. Wear loose-fitting clothes.
6. Patient allowed to rest hands on RW, must not push down or pull.
7. Instructed in cross leg technique or knee to chest to donn/doff LE garments.
8. Keep reaching activities within BOS.
9. Use flex foam tube to manipulate curvature, place comb or brush inside in order to reach back of head.
10. Instruct in work simplification: place items in kitchen within reach, nothing too high or too low.
11. Instruct in timed interval exercises vs reps after 2-4 weeks post-op *(don't forget to grade the activity appropriately).

Documentation:

Ther-ex: 97110

1. Patient utilized omnicycle (cardiac mode) for 15 minutes seated x 2 one-minute rest break with an activity performance of 55% in order to increase endurance, improve management of self-care tasks and strength, pursed lip breathing emphasized during endurance training activity.

Ther Act: 97530

3. Patient participated in tabletop card stacking activity w/o AD while standing on an uneven surface (foam pad) CGA, tolerating 2 minutes @ a time upon needing to sit. Pt guided through deep breathing in order to decrease the risk of SOB and educated on maintaining an erect posture to support respiration.

Therapeutic Exercises: The best exercise is focused exercise.

HAND

1. Finger lifts:
   Place hand down flat on the table (palm down). Lift each finger off the table and hold it up for a few seconds. Exercise just one finger at a time.
   Using hand web or a small rubber band can provide resistance

   Benefits: typing, using a computer mouse, managing perfume spray bottle, pressing numbers on the microwave

2. Finger add/abduction:
   Spread fingers w/ increased intensity using rubber band.
   Put hand flat on a table (palm down) and practice spreading fingers apart and then bring them back together.

   Benefits: holding a glass, wiping counter/mirror

3. Hand strengthening:
   - Digiflex
   - Grip/squeeze ball
   - Use thera-putty for resistance and strengthening
   - Hand web exercises
   - Use dynamometer to measure hand strength

4. Finger Opposition

   Benefits: fasteners-clips, picking up coins, twisting off caps

WRIST

1. Hang weak wrist over the table edge, place the stronger hand over the weak hand and stretch it towards the floor.

2. Standing at the edge of the table with both hands (palms facing down), lean forward to stretch.

3. Seated, forearm on the table (pronation) holding cone or weight over the table edge, turn wrist so the palm hand is facing up, then return towards the floor (palm down).

   Benefits: pouring milk, juice pitcher

4. Wrist flexion/extension: Hang wrist over the table, make a fist, flex upward toward the ceiling then downward toward the floor, incorporate dumbbell for additional resistance.

   Benefits: washing dishes, lifting cup/item

5. Supination & Pronation with or w/o weight

   Benefits: holding soup, using utensils, writing

6. Interlock fingers, slowly bend wrist towards you then away (ulnar/radial deviation)

   Benefits: turn knob on the door, key in the door

ARMS

1. Triceps:

Benefits: facilitates rise/sit in a chair

- Wheelchair dip/push-ups

- Modified close grip chest press (seated, elbows flexed to 90" angle holding dowel, push forward until elbow is straight, keep elbows close to the body, keep dowel below chest height)
- Overhead triceps extension (can use pulley, dumbbell or theraband, arm 180" flexed, hand to ceiling, bend @ elbow then extend to ceiling)
- Triceps kickbacks (bend forward stand on sitting, w/c armrest removed, arm to side, hyper-extension holding dumbbell palm to ceiling)

2. Core Strengthening:

Benefits: postural control, dynamic sitting balance, and prevention of leaning

- Side Bends (hold weight in one hand along the side of the body, arms parallel to hips, slowly bend side towards right/left sides lowering weight towards the floor)
- Dynamic bending (holding dowel or dumbbell), flex trunk while lowering weight towards ankle then return to starting position, repeat
- Sit-ups, seated on therapy mat or EOB, grade accordingly
- Trunk rotation holding the dowel.

3. Shoulder flexion/extension: Using wrist weight, dowel bar or dumbbells

   Benefits: increase functional reach, using a mop, broom, cleaning, and dressing etc.

   - Basic shoulder flexion/extension

4. Modified shoulder flexion/extension in gravity lessened position

5. Shoulder external/internal rotation: should be done in a supine position or seated using theraband or dumbbell

   Benefits: straightening collar, comb back of hair, fasten bra, tucking shirt into pants etc.
   - *Complete in supine, seated or on therapy mat*

6. Biceps:
   Benefits: self-feeding, hygiene/grooming, UBD etc.
   - Basic elbow flexion/extension in supination, then pronation
   - Hammer bicep curls

7. Scapular protraction/retraction:
   Benefits: opening closet, carrying object (laundry basket), pulling
   - Standing up or seated, leaning forward: reach/extend arm out in front of you then pull arm back as to pinch shoulder blades together.

How to motivate the unmotivated?

There are factors that must be addressed to find out the underlying causes of poor motivation, lack of interest, failure to thrive, being uncooperative, detached, and all the other terms we therapist's use to describe a patient unwilling to participate in the therapy.

By analyzing these 3 compromised areas;

1) Emotional health
2) External factors
3) Misunderstood rehabilitation expectation

These areas provide a means of approach when dealing with difficult patients.

Tips to remember:

- Get down to their eye level (don't stand over).
- Speak slowly and calmly.
- You are dealing with adults, not children, always be respectful.
- Always introduce yourself first with a smile.
- Be aware of body language (crossing arms, rolling eyes, posture).

<u>Emotional health</u>:

1. Is your patient sad, if so why?

   1st Listen to your patient attentively.

   2nd Show empathy.

   3rd Ask the patient, what can I do to help?

   4th Provide a solution while explaining how your services and participation in the therapy is beneficial.

   5th Keep your word and follow through.

2. Is your patient mad, if so why?

   1st Listen to your patient attentively.

   2nd Use phrases like, “I am sorry”, “I understand how that can be frustrating”, “You are right”.

   3rdAfter listening to your patient, ask if there is anything you can do to help, if no. Leave the room stating, “I will give you some time and will revisit you later”. When someone is upset, they are not thinking clearly so it’s best to give them some space in order to calm down.

   4th Once you return to the room, ask the patient how they are feeling, wait for an answer vs assuming everything is better.

   5th Provide a positive outlook of the situation.

   6th Change the topic, e.g. comment on a commercial or TV show that is on in the patient’s room, or a picture that is on the wall.

   7th Express how beneficial therapy is and how you would appreciate their participation.

   8th Show gratitude, e.g. “I appreciate you trying”.

3. Is your patient depressed, if so why?

   1st Be careful of your body language.

   2nd Be kind with your words and not forceful.

   3rd Use phrases like, “whatever you are feeling, I’m here to help” in order to gain trust.

   4th Initiate with straightforward and basic activities such as ADLs, (light grooming, dressing, EOB sitting while talking) etc.

   5th Be patient.

4. Is your patient frustrated, if so why?

   1st Listen to their concerns attentively.

2nd "I understand your frustration" use validation as appropriate.
3rd Find out why they are frustrated, is their functional improvements slower than expected? Is it a problem with nursing care? Is the food not tasty? etc.
4th Provide solutions and redirect thoughts towards therapy goals.

5. Does your patient have obsessive-compulsive behavior which affects participation?
   1st It is always best to tell your patient what you are doing before you do it. Always introduce yourself and the activity explaining the reason and the benefit of doing it.
   2nd Find out what bothers them and what they prefer.
   3rd Look for signs of anxiety in order to grade activities to facilitate success.
   4th Provide tasks where your patient feels as if they have control.

6. Is your patient bored, if so why?
   1st Find out why your patient is bored. Is it the exercise? Is it the facility? Are the activities not challenging enough etc.?
   2nd Once you have your "why" answered, create unique and challenging activities while educating them on the benefits and importance of participating in skilled OT services.

We must remember when you are angry, sad, or in pain, the last thing you want to hear is let's go to "work". Yes, I said "work" because this is what comes to mind for most patients when they are in an unmotivated state. I can only speak from experience. I have applied these strategies and have achieved 90% success in getting my patients to cooperate. I think at times we forget that we are dealing with human beings and not animals. Individuals who are fighting against the disease, trying to recover after injury, surgery or loss of independence are looking for someone to understand and relate.

External Factors:

External factors can influence recovery and motivation. External factors entail possible housing loss, overdue bills, rocky relationships with spouse, friend or children, lack of MD following up an appointment to name a few. External factors are out of our control, but we can remind patients on the importance of complete therapy in order to be d/c sooner than later in order to be able to return to PLOF safely. I always tell my patients "it's best to get the job done now, instead of returning home too soon and then have to come back". Once you educate your patient's on the importance of showing progress and requirements for d/c, it tends to motive them, well in most cases.

Misunderstood rehabilitation expectation:

We are professionals. So our communication with our patients should reflect our knowledge and expertise. If a patient is poorly educated on goals, POC, and estimated d/c plans, they won't understand rehab expectation. It is important to ask your patient upon encounter, "what are your goals for therapy?" By knowing their needs, you can describe your requirements in order to achieve their goal. It is also important to communicate with nursing and the social worker regarding patient and therapy expectation for added support for rehabilitation participation. Remember communication is key!

Unfortunate situations:

If your patient is refusing therapy because of pain, inform nursing and provide pain modalities as appropriate. Patient's may refuse therapy due to pain/illness. It is important not to force a patient. Here is my four-step approach to this unfortunate situation.

1st Ask the patient what is wrong. (A headache, pain, stomach upset etc.), please note "tired" is not an acceptable refusal, but a patient returning from dialysis stating they are "tired" is more acceptable which I will address later. Always show empathy.

2nd Ask the patient, "was nursing notified of your complaints?" If no, go to nursing and explain the situation and if yes, ask the patient if anything was provided.

3rd Patient's have a tendency to not inform nursing. So allow some time for pain medication, headache pill etc. but before leaving the room, don't forget to let your patient know you will be returning soon.

4th Remind your patient of therapy expectation. You can also have nursing back you up. Again, "DON'T BE FORCEFUL". Use phrases like, "Let's try to do a little something", "We will do as much as you can tolerate", "We can take a lot of rest breaks if you need it", "Please try your best, I would appreciate it". "Therapy is your ticket home; you don't want to stay here longer than you have to".

These motivational tips are just what I call them, "tips". It is not a 100% guarantee that your patients will participate in therapy every time. This is just what I used and have seen more success than refusals. To be honest, some patients are just lazy and prefer to stay in bed claiming to be tired or ill. I did say some, there are some exceptions like dialysis patients who are genuinely tired. So you must use your critical thinking/reasoning skills to analyze every situation. It is our job to motivate the unmotivated, but you will win some and lose some and that is ok. We are not drill sergeants. Our goal is to restore, facilitate, adapt, teach, advocate and motivate in order to provide the opportunity for every patient to have quality of life after the disease, illness, and injury.

Food for thought!

Scenario Case #1:

John is a 56-year-old male who was admitted into your rehabilitation facility and underwent laminectomy surgery after years of suffering from spinal stenosis. John was in rehabilitation for 2-months at another facility before he was transported to yours. John requires Max Ax2 for transfers in/out of bed, total dependent for toileting, performs LB dressing in supine with Max A and complains of poor tactile sensation in legs and pins and needles in feet. John wears a back brace OOB at all times. Due to poor quadriceps strength during sit to stand training, John requires Max Ax2 at parallel bars with bilateral knees supported to decrease flexion and tactile cueing for reducing hyperextension. John has been in your facility now for 4-weeks with no follow-up MD appointment in sight. The only changes in his overall functional performance are static/dynamic sitting balance and UE strength. You knock before entering his room. John is lying in bed, shades closed, lights off, television off even though it is a hot summer day. In a monotone voice with no eye contact when asked what time he wanted therapy, John responds, "I don't want therapy today".

What do you do? Use this case scenario to problem solve and critically think on how you can motivate John to participate with his skilled OT services. What compromised area does John's case fall under and how would you address this matter? This is a great in-class case study assignment, group discussion activity, or personal critical thinking challenge.

I hope this book was helpful, any feedback is appreciated. I can be reached at Timisha.daniels@gmail.com and YouTube under Timisha Tross. Thank you!

23005920R00059

Printed in Great Britain
by Amazon